AN INTRODUCTION

TO

PUBLIC LAW

KEITH J. EDDEY, B.A.

*Solicitor of the Supreme Court; Senior Lecturer in Law and
Local Government, Oxford College of Technology*

LONDON
BUTTERWORTHS
1967

ENGLAND:	BUTTERWORTH & CO. (PUBLISHERS) LTD.
	LONDON: 88 KINGSWAY, W.C.2
AUSTRALIA:	BUTTERWORTH & CO. (AUSTRALIA) LTD.
	SYDNEY: 20 LOFTUS STREET
	MELBOURNE: 473 BOURKE STREET
	BRISBANE: 240 QUEEN STREET
CANADA:	BUTTERWORTH & CO. (CANADA) LTD.
	TORONTO: 14 CURITY AVENUE, 16
NEW ZEALAND:	BUTTERWORTH & CO. (NEW ZEALAND) LTD.
	WELLINGTON: 49/51 BALLANCE STREET
	AUCKLAND: 35 HIGH STREET
SOUTH AFRICA:	BUTTERWORTH & CO. (SOUTH AFRICA) LTD.
	DURBAN: 33/35 BEACH GROVE

Printed in Great Britain by R. J. Acford Ltd., Industrial Estate, Chichester, Sussex

Preface

This book is intended to assist Local Government Officers who are preparing for the Local Government Examinations Board Intermediate Examination in the subject "Elements of Public Law". It is hoped that it will also serve as introductory reading for University Degree students beginning a study of English Law before they are called upon to master the complexities of the advanced text-books on Constitutional and Administrative Law.

Having had several years' experience of teaching Local Government Officers, I have been aware throughout the writing of the book that the students for whom it is primarily intended come to the subject without having studied Law before. I have therefore tried to present the material in as elementary a way as the subject permits; for the same reason I have not thought it necessary to supply footnotes or detailed references.

At least one advantage follows from the fact that the book has to cover the syllabus published by the Local Government Examinations Board. The author's topics are prescribed for him and he can thus evade the need to defend the choice made. The balance of the treatment is however the author's responsibility and here I have tried to produce a simple pattern emphasising throughout the highly practical nature of this field of law, whilst the use wherever possible of recent cases and statutes stresses its topicality.

From the time when the Publishers invited me to write this book they have been of great help which has included the provision of the Index and the Tables of Cases and Statutes and permitting me to quote extracts from the *All England Law Reports*.

Any text-book must owe a debt to previous text-book writers in the same and related fields and this I readily acknowledge. In addition I must record a substantial debt to my students who, by their stimulating criticism and enquiries over the years, have considerably increased my own appreciation and enjoyment of the legal subjects which I teach. I am also most grateful to my wife who typed the manuscript.

CUMNOR,   KEITH EDDEY
  OXFORD.
September, 1967.

Contents

INDEX

Table of Statutes

References to "Stats." are to Halsbury's Statutes (Second Edn.) showing the volume and page at which the annotated text of the Act will be found.

Table of Cases

Chapter I

The Law of England

I INTRODUCTION

The purpose of this chapter is to provide some of the basic information about English law which the reader must have in order to proceed to a consideration of the one branch, public law, which is the subject of this book.

Since every institution in the English legal system is the result of a continuous process of history a brief survey will be made, at the start, of the most important historical factors which have contributed to the development of English law. Summarised as this survey must be, it will nevertheless serve to emphasise the almost unbroken progression of English law over a thousand years and so establish an awareness of the long history not only of the courts and the legal profession but also of the principles of law which, as gradually established over the centuries, have now been built up into the different branches of law.

These various branches or categories of law with the more important of their customary divisions will then be briefly considered and an attempt will be made to fit public law into its place in the system. This section will endeavour to explain what is included within the term "public law", a task by no means easy because, strictly, English law recognises no such category.

As in all fields of law the actual cases which give rise to so many of the principles in force are a vital field of study. The part played by the courts in this way in the making of law will be reserved to chapter 3 for full consideration, but an explanation of the work of the lawyers, and of the facilities now available to persons in financial need of "legal aid and advice" would seem to be appropriate even at this early stage.

The chapter will end with a consideration of a most important topic, the sources of English law. Whatever field of law is in question there are always certain sources from which the law is derived. The term source means in this context the authority for the proposition

stated as law: a source is an answer to the question, how does one
know that a particular principle is the law. For example, where is it
actually stipulated in law that a car driver must not exceed 70 miles
per hour? Where is the law that requires that such a driver must be
insured against certain risks? If, through bad driving, he injures a
pedestrian how is it that one can be virtually sure that the driver
will have to pay the pedestrian compensation? In each case the
answer will be a "source" of law and will be found discussed in the
final section of the chapter.

2   THE NATURE AND DEVELOPMENT OF ENGLISH LAW

(a) The Nature of English Law

(i) *Absence of a written code.*—Just as the present system of Government in England is the outcome of centuries of English history so
English law also is the result of a gradual development over hundreds
of years.   The student of English law is inevitably the student of
English history because the former can only be fully intelligible in
the light of the latter.   The law of England is the product of the
history of England: thus great antiquity and continuity are both
inescapable and fundamental characteristics of it.

In the same way, just as there has never been a written constitution
devised as a guide to the system of government neither has there ever
been a successful attempt to produce in written form the law of
England. Thus another of the outstanding characteristics of English
law, unlike the position prevailing on the continent, is that in no
major branch of the law is it possible to purchase a complete documentary code.   Instead the process of continuous decision by the
judges has resulted in each branch of the law being built up on the
basis of decided cases.   Acts of Parliament have contributed much
too, but there are important fields of law where even today legislation
is of minor importance.   Moreover in those fields of law where
legislation is relevant, for example company law in the Companies
Act 1948, the need for interpretation of words and phrases by the
judges leads to their making a major contribution to the development of the subject.   And this development is never-ending so that
in all branches of the law the student is faced with the problem of
continuing change.   The vital part played by the judges is, like the
contribution of legislation, a matter which will receive fuller consideration in the section on sources of public law later in this
chapter.

(ii) *Influence of Roman law.*—Another way in which English law differs from the law of many continental countries is in its native development free from the introduction of the principles of Roman law. The explanation again lies in the antiquity and continuity referred to above whereby no need for the introduction of such principles was ever felt to be necessary. It is true that in the Probate Divorce and Admiralty Division of the High Court one can trace the influence of Roman law affecting English law through the church courts and through the law of merchants trading internationally, but broadly speaking the Roman law influence is not widely apparent. Instead English law has always retained its links with the feudal system of medieval England. For example, the rule that the eldest son inherited his deceased father's estate only finally went out in the Administration of Estates Act 1925, at the same time as the complicated land law which was built up on the basis of the feudal tenures and estates was simplified by the Law of Property Act 1925.

(iii) *The role of laymen in the legal system.*—In addition to these factors which go some way towards throwing light on the nature of English law there are a number of other rather more practical considerations which are also relevant. For example very great stress has always been placed on the use of laymen in the system with the intention that the law should never be allowed to become remote from "the man in the street". For this reason in all serious criminal offences the accused person, if he pleads "not guilty", is entitled to be tried by twelve of his fellow-countrymen. Called "the jury" they are to be the judges of the matters of fact in dispute and it will be their verdict which will "convict" or "acquit" the accused person. In certain civil cases a jury is possible too; in particular where an injury to a person's reputation is alleged in defamation proceedings, *i.e.* in one of the two forms of defamation known as libel and slander. With only limited exceptions, such as clergymen and lawyers, all householders between the ages of 21 and 60 are eligible to serve on a jury and this means that in the course of a year a vast number of the general public are actively associated with one of the most important aspects of the process of law. In another important respect also, laymen play a vital part in the system. This is as magistrates, or justices of the peace, of whom there are in total some 16,000. Magistrates deal with the vast majority of criminal cases in their "court of summary jurisdiction" where they hear, determine and sentence for minor offences. In a second quite different capacity they hold a preliminary enquiry into the more serious criminal offences to discover whether or not the prosecution can make out a *"prima facie"* (at first sight) case against the accused person and if so to commit him for trial. Magistrates also have a useful role in certain civil cases. Thus in this way too, laymen are closely associated with the law and this is a valuable asset in helping to ensure that the law does not lose touch with the views of the persons it is intended to protect.

(iv) *The independence of the judiciary.*—Another feature of English law is the very real effort which is made to secure the independence of the judiciary. The object is to see that the judges are encouraged to be as independent and unprejudiced in their approach to a case as is possible. Thus the judges in England are always selected from the ranks of the existing barristers. The result is that every judge will have had years of experience as an advocate in the courts before becoming a judge. This is in contrast to systems elsewhere under which judges are a part of the civil service and train for judgeship as for a career. Furthermore for reasons of history considerable stress has for long been laid on keeping judges free from any possible influence by the government of the day. For this reason politics do not affect appointments and, once appointed, a judge cannot easily be dismissed from office. Dismissal can only be brought about by a petition by both Houses of Parliament to the Monarch requesting the dismissal and such action has never been necessary yet. By similar reasoning the salaries of judges are not subject to annual review by Parliament and by another convention the decisions of particular judges are not criticised other than in general terms in Parliament. To discourage any attempt to win the favour of the government of the day in order to obtain promotion, the salaries of the High Court judges and the Court of Appeal judges are identical at £10,000 per annum. Yet despite all these important factors perhaps the most important influence in the independence of the judges lies in the tradition of the English Bar which has cultivated throughout a long history enormous respect for the proper application of the law and an independence of mind in the individual barrister which has long served the law and the nation in good stead.

(v) *The position of the police.*—Another peculiarly English institution is the police service. Responsible as the police are for law and order they are nonetheless very strictly subject to the law and, as chapter 6 will show, the powers which they have are carefully balanced, some would say too carefully balanced, against the undue restriction of the liberties of the subject. The police officer is neither a civil servant nor a local government officer although he is employed by a local authority and is paid partly from local and partly from national funds. In many respects his legal powers are identical to those of the individual citizen and there is nothing of the bullying power-conscious tough guy about the English policeman. If he makes a mistake he can all too easily be sued, depending on the circumstances, for wrongful arrest, assault and battery or even malicious prosecution since he has no special immunity in law.

The reason why the police are so strictly curtailed under the law is because of another vital feature of English law which is the emphasis laid on the liberty of the subject. Personal liberty is the highest valued right an English subject has, and together with the various rights associated with personal liberty, such as freedom of speech, and freedom to attend public meetings, these are considered of such importance to English law that, in a sense, everything in English public law is intended to confirm these rights to the individual. Hence, in part, the difficult role of the police officer; all the law's presumptions are against him.

(vi) *Summary.*—A study of the nature or characteristics of English law will need to include the following factors which have been outlined above:

  (i) antiquity and continuity
 (ii) the absence of documentary codes and the importance of actual case decisions
(iii) the absence of Roman law principles
(iv) the association of laymen with the law
 (v) the independence of the judiciary
(vi) the role of the police service.

(b) The development of English law

(i) *The early court system.*—The earliest known English law goes back to the centuries before the Norman conquest when the Anglo-Saxons were the ruling force in the country. To be accurate these laws which were written in the Anglo-Saxon language go back to the time when England as a national entity had yet to emerge. Thus they are the law as then applied in a particular part of this country. It is only after the Norman conquest in 1066 that it would be true to say that there is a "law of England" and even then it would be only generally true. With the passage of time the government became a national government and, in consequence, the legal system and the enforcement of law became a national system also.

The court system of these early days consisted of the King's courts in London providing royal justice and for the more trivial local matters feudal courts based locally and administered through the leading local land-owner. From an early date the King would send his judges around the country in order to try the more serious criminal matters. This the judges would do at the assize towns, the most important boroughs in the country, thus beginning a system which has continued through the centuries and remains in being today. For civil matters, however, cases had to be brought at Westminster. As the King's courts grew in effectiveness so more and more people sought for royal justice and, since the Monarch enjoyed the profit from the activities of the courts, he was keen to encourage this development.

To understand the position of the King's courts in these early times it is necessary to think of the difficulties in trying to enforce law and order on the King's behalf throughout the length and breadth of England at a time when many obstacles existed to this end. Local magnates were not anxious to lose the profits derived from cases heard in their own courts and bad communications made it difficult to enforce in the outlying districts judgments obtained in London. An additional problem for the judges in these early times was that because a national law was a new concept they were frequently asked to give decisions based on the local custom of the area. So from an early date the judges collaborated in order to lay down the law on a national basis—law which although often based in origin on custom was nevertheless to be "common" to all the country. Hence this law became known as the "common law" and the courts as the "common law courts".

(ii) *The King's Courts.*—There were three of these royal courts. There was one which dealt with disputes in which the King himself had an interest, the Court of King's Bench; another concerned itself with matters concerning the royal revenue, the Court of Exchequer; and finally the third took, for a fee, cases which involved the King's subjects, the Court of Common Pleas. These courts expanded their respective jurisdictions as the centuries passed and they remained a prominent feature of the English legal system until 1880 when the three were merged to form one division of the High Court of Justice, now the Queen's Bench Division.

(iii) *The beginning of Equity.*—The rapid growth of business in medieval times of these courts not only led to the establishment of a "common law" but also caused the courts to become very rigid in their procedure. The procedure laid down for the bringing of civil cases required the use of writs or forms of action; that is whenever a person desired to make a claim he had to present his case on the basis of an existing writ. In most cases this was un-objectionable, but where a person had a claim which was not known to the law under the existing writ system then the common law judges refused to assist him thus giving rise to the maxim "no writ, no remedy". This state of affairs led to such obvious injustice that dissatisfied claimants took to petitioning the King in person asking for his intervention to give them justice. The King passed the petitions to the Lord High Chancellor, who at the time was usually an ecclesiastic and known as "the keeper of the King's conscience". The Lord High Chancellor charged with the responsibility for "letting right be done", found it necessary to establish his own court, called the Court of Chancery, and in this court he would sit to give decisions based on fairness, or as it came to be called "in equity". This was the origin of the court of equity and of the system of law known as equity. The practice seems to date from about the middle of the fourteenth century but soon it developed into a formal court headed by a Lord Chancellor who, as at present, was the most eminent lawyer of his day. An early criticism of the equity court was that since the matter was left entirely to the discretion of the Lord Chancellor the decision given tended to vary according to the Chancellor's conscience or the Chancellor's foot! But in time this criticism lost its validity because later Lord Chancellors would allow themselves to be guided as to the equity principles to be applied by the decisions of their predecessors. They thus came to place as much emphasis on previous case decisions (precedents) as did the common law judges (see later in this chapter—Sources of English law: case law).

(iv) *Common Law and Equity.*—The development of the Court of Chancery meant that for some five hundred years the English legal system contained two separate branches of law, equity and common law, each with its own courts and its own remedies. Although equity saw itself as a gloss or supplement to the common law nonetheless it worked quite independently of it and each system built up its case law over the years into a formidable collection of precedents. However the unsatisfactory basis of this dual arrangement became increasingly apparent, particularly where circumstances involved actions being pursued in both sets of courts at once. In the Judicature Acts 1873–1875 the two systems were merged into a new High Court of Justice with the equity branch forming one of the divisions as the Chancery Division of the High Court. These Acts abolished the separate jurisdictions and laid down that all judges should be able to give common law and equity remedies as necessary: where however the principles conflicted, those of equity were to prevail. One result of the merger is that today in a claim it is possible to sue for damages (the common law remedy) and an injunction (the equity remedy) in the same action and in the same court. It is still necessary to know the old equity and common law reasoning nonetheless, because the judge will apply the various principles on the basis of the former systems. For example, whereas a common law remedy was given as of right, an equity remedy always lay within the discretion of the judge and would only be granted if certain conditions were fulfilled. This is one reason why it remains essential for lawyers to know the former law since without such detailed study they would not understand the present position.

3 THE PRINCIPAL BRANCHES OF ENGLISH LAW

English law is divided into two fundamental categories. Criminal law and civil law.

(a) Criminal Law

Most States make this distinction drawing a line between misconduct which is regarded as affecting the public at large and misconduct which affects only the particular individuals concerned with it. The law provides remedies in both categories but in the first kind of misconduct the State intervenes on the public's behalf to play the role of prosecutor. If a person steals, his misconduct might at first sight appear to affect only the person who is the loser, but a moment's reflection will show that such misconduct indirectly affects a large number of the public. It may lead to further stealing, to breaches of the peace, mob law and noose trial and rather than have this state of affairs such misconduct is treated as an offence against the community or to use the better known term, as a crime. Thus the State through the Crown initiates most prosecutions and so such trial cases are known as *R*. v. *Smith* (the name of the accused person), the R standing for Rex (latin: King) or Regina (latin: Queen). Because the sanctions involved may result in the person prosecuted being deprived of his personal liberty it has long been the custom for such cases to be tried in special criminal courts under a carefully devised procedure intended to give the accused person a fair trial. In chapter 3 a full examination of these courts and their procedure will be made. At this point it is only necessary to stress that the fundamental rule in all criminal cases is that the accused person is presumed innocent of the crime charged until the prosecution have proved him guilty beyond all reasonable doubt.

(i) *The definition of crime.*—As to what sort of misconduct constitutes a crime, this will depend on the views of the society of the time. Some misconduct will clearly be regarded as criminal in all ages—all forms of homicide for example, robbery and theft—but at the present time suggestions are rife that certain conduct now criminal should be made lawful. It is felt that subject to certain conditions that, for example, homosexual acts between consenting adults and, as a second example, the carrying out of an abortion again subject to certain conditions, should no longer be treated as crimes. Similarly the sanctions imposed in criminal law, a monetary fine or imprisonment, will vary in severity from age to age. In the eighteenth century hanging was taken to be an appropriate punishment for a wide range of offences, the proof of which today would involve a monetary fine only. The present age has, for instance, by the Murder (Abolition of Death Penalty) Act 1965 seen fit to do without capital punishment for murder for an experimental five year period.

Crimes may be classified in two ways. The old method was to distinguish between treason, felony and misdemeanour. A treason is an offence against the security of the State by technically breaking the allegiance owed to the Crown. The Statute of Treason 1351 specified seven possible forms of the offence of which the two afterwards most used were "levying war against the Queen in her realm" and "adhering to the Queen's enemies in her realm by giving to them aid and comfort in the realm or elsewhere". A felony is any offence, at common law or by statute, a conviction for which resulted in a forfeiture of land and/or goods to the Crown. Naturally these felonies tended to be the more serious crimes; all other crimes, which were neither treason nor felony, were called misdemeanours. The dividing line between felony and misdemeanour was never a sound one and since the forfeiture of property for treason and felony was formally abolished by the Forfeiture Act 1870 the distinction was difficult to justify. Accordingly it was abolished by the Criminal Law Act 1967. This Act introduced a new distinction between "arrestable" offences (for which a person may be arrested without warrant) and other offences. Arrestable offences are those for which a person is liable to imprisonment for five years or more.

The alternative classification is to distinguish between crimes triable only on "indictment" at Quarter Sessions or Assizes and those triable "summarily" before magistrates. (The work of the courts involved will be explained in chapter 3). Summary offences are comparatively minor in significance whereas all the more serious crimes fall into the indictable category. Even under this classification however confusion occurs because there is an overlap between the two classes of offence in that some indictable offences can be tried summarily at the accused person's request.

(b) Civil law

All branches of law which do not fall within criminal law are branches of the Civil law. These include the law of contract and the law of tort, the law concerning property and succession, family law and constitutional and administrative law. Such vast fields of law have so little in common that it is difficult to find any factor which links them together. Perhaps the best approach is to say that in all these various fields of law the State lays down rules which assist the individual parties in knowing their rights and obligations in relation to each other.

(i) *The law of contract.*—The law of contract is designed to ensure that persons who enter into an agreement with each other are then bound to carry out that agreement on pain of having to pay compensation to the person injured by the default. The law, that is, will intervene to force parties to honour their contracts. On the other hand it is not every agreement that the law will enforce, but only those where the parties, either expressly or by implication, intended the agreement to be legally binding. In addition there are a whole range of matters that can affect the validity of a contract such as the age and state of mind of the parties, whether the consent of the parties was genuinely given in the making of the agreement and whether an Act of Parliament, or a judge's rule of public policy, affects the legality of the agreement made.

Over the years the courts have built up a large number of principles from the thousands of cases which they have been called upon to decide. Hence the law of contract is not found in the form of a documentary code but in the principles established by the judges from the cases over the years; and with each month that passes new cases are heard and decided and these in turn add to or qualify the existing law.

Typical examples of contracts entered into every day are, the purchase of goods from a shop, a contract of carriage by bus or train and the building of or sale of a house. Despite the laymen's view to the contrary, there is, in general, no need for the contract to be made in writing; it can be, and frequently is, made verbally.

(ii) *The law of tort.*—The law of tort is concerned with misconduct which the law is prepared to regard as "wrong" in the sense that it will require compensation to be paid to a person who has suffered loss as a result of this "wrong". The word "tort" is Norman-French and means "twisted" and therefore "wrong". The misconduct involved need not be a criminal act, for example trespassing on the land of a local farmer whilst picnicking is not a criminal act, but it is the tort of trespass to land. Similarly a frequent misuse of property by causing undue noise, which makes for considerable inconvenience for the person occupying the adjoining house, is the tort of nuisance, but such misconduct is not a crime. On the other hand, some acts of misconduct can constitute both a tort and a crime. A theft, for example, is both the crime of larceny and its civil counterpart, the tort of conversion.

So far as the law of tort is concerned the main theme throughout is that the law is willing to provide a monetary remedy for any one suffering loss as a result of conduct which the law recognises as wrongful. The loss may arise through personal injuries sustained as a result of a negligent act by a car driver or by a fellow worker, or it may be a loss of reputation through some libel or slander made public and injuring the character of the person concerned, or again it may be a gross inconvenience suffered in the enjoyment of property or it can be a direct financial loss caused by someone deliberately "passing off" his goods as if they were those of the person complaining. In each case compensation, in the form of damages, will be awarded.

There are a number of torts known to the law, of which the most important are: negligence, nuisance, trespass and defamation. However the categories of tort are never closed and it is always open to the courts to treat some particular form of conduct as tortious. For example in the case of *Rookes* v. *Barnard* in 1964, some trade union members were held liable to an ex-member whose employment they had improperly caused to be terminated. The tort found to have been committed here was one of which little had been heard for many years, the tort of "intimidation". Although Parliament has now changed the law as it relates to trade unionists by the Trade Disputes Act 1965, the tort of "intimidation" remains.

It will be noticed that the law of contract can be distinguished from the law of tort in that in a contract the parties have themselves voluntarily entered into the rights and obligations involved; whereas in a case of tort the parties may be quite unknown to each other, the legal relationship between them having been imposed upon them by the law. Like the law of contract, however, the law of tort has been built up on the basis of actual decided cases and there is no documentary code on the subject. The principles of tort have been extracted from the cases and legislation affecting the subject is negligible.

(iii) *The law of property.*—The law of property is a complex subject because considerable stress is laid on the technical legal rights which can exist in the ownership of land and of personal property. The interests which can exist in one piece of land at any time are manifold. The following are just some of such interests: the freeholder, the leaseholder, trustees, the beneficiary, the lodger, the executor or the administrator, the life tenant, joint owners (co-owners), the person who has a right of way over the property, the person who enjoys the benefit of a restrictive covenant affecting the property, the person who has lent money on the security of the property (the mortgagee). It is thus not difficult to understand that the transfer of land or of these interests in land is a complicated process and requires a special legal skill which is known as "conveyancing". Consequently there are two fields of study; the law of property, which is concerned with what these interests are, how they are created and their status in relation to each other, and conveyancing which is only concerned with the actual transfer of these interests.

Taking the word "property" in its broadest sense, the field of study extends beyond land, or real property, to cover the law of personal property concerned as it is with the ownership of the various forms of personal property, and of the way in which the transfer of the ownership of such property can take place. It is one thing to transfer the ownership of a typewriter, another thing a car, and another thing again to transfer a debt or the right to redeem a pawn or a pledge. In particular this subject includes the law of hire-purchase which is a complex matter constantly affected by new legislation.

(iv) *The law of succession.*—The law of succession deals with the passing of property, land and personal effects, on a death. It is thus concerned with the making of a valid will, which is the document which appoints a representative to carry out the last wishes, as there expressed, of the deceased person. As might be expected the importance of such a document causes it to be carefully examined and construed in law before effect will be given to it. In fact the High Court through the Probate Divorce and Admiralty Division, will insist on a will being authenticated or "proved" immediately after the death and before the person appointed proceeds to wind up the estate. Such a person appointed under a will is called an executor.

Where a person dies without having made a will it will still be necessary for his estate to be dealt with and so the High Court will have to approve the appointment of administrators. Usually the closest relatives of the deceased become these administrators and they will deal with the estate and then distribute the balance available in accordance with rules laid down by Act of Parliament. These rules are intended to do for the deceased what he has failed to do for himself through not making a will and they are based on the assumption that most persons would wish their next-of-kin to benefit.

The High Court in each instance provides documentary proof of its authentication by issuing in the case of a will being left, a probate, and where no will has been left, letters of administration. Executors and administrators have to produce these documents as proof of their authority to deal with the deceased person's estate.

If a dispute occurs over the validity of a will, for example whether it has been properly signed and witnessed, then the probate branch of the High Court will hear evidence and decide whether or not to grant probate of the will in question. If, however, the dispute concerns the meaning of words or phrases used in the will then the Chancery Division of the High Court will give a ruling on the interpretation in dispute.

In order to make applications for probate or letters of administration easier the High Court has established a number of probate registries in large towns in England and Wales.

(v) *Family law.*—Family law includes a study of such matters as the requirements for a valid marriage, the grounds on which a nullity decree may be obtained, and the grounds on which a decree of dissolution of marriage (divorce) may be granted. It is also concerned with the various ensuing rights and obligations as to maintenance, and the welfare and custody of the children of the marriage.

Under this same heading will also come the law with regard to the property rights and obligations of a husband and wife and the relationship of parent and child. This latter heading will extend to cover the guardianship of infants, the making of affiliation orders requiring the alleged father to support an illegitimate child, adoption orders, legitimation orders and matters arising under the legislation affecting children and young persons. All told this is a vast field of law of considerable complexity.

4 PUBLIC LAW

The previous section has considered the principal branches of English law, following the widely accepted division of these branches into criminal and civil law. This division is easily justified since England has a separate system of civil and criminal courts and in these courts two quite different forms of procedure are followed. The division is thus fundamental.

However it is also possible to suggest another division of these branches of English law and this would be into private law and public law. Private law would cover the fields of law in which individuals are in conflict with other individuals thus including contract, tort, property, succession and family law. Public law would be concerned with those fields of law where the individual is concerned with the government of the State and this would include constitutional and administrative law and also criminal law. Public law, as so defined, is thus made up of a mixture of civil and criminal law.

(a) Criminal law

Dealing first with the criminal law it is clear that every crime as declared by the State is a matter of public law since each member of the public is affected by it. However, as might be expected, the field of criminal law is so vast that for anything like an adequate treatment it would require a book to itself. On that basis no more than a hint can be given here of the sort of conduct which the State has made punishable as crimes. As a general rule a criminal act can be said to involve two elements, *"actus reus"* (a guilty act) and *"mens rea"* (a guilty mind)—and both must occur together for a criminal offence to be committed. There are qualifications to this, but in the main this statement is still true. One cannot be convicted of a crime unless the two are in combination, the full maxim is *"actus non facit reum nisi mens sit rea"*—an act does not make the person guilty unless the mind is guilty.

Misconduct which is today classed as criminal can be grouped in the following way:

(i) *Crimes against the person.*—The most serious is murder, the essence of which is "killing with malice aforethought"; if there is no "malice aforethought" then the crime is the lesser offence of "unlawfully killing", or manslaughter. All forms of taking life are known as homicide; even the now most common one of "causing death by dangerous driving".

Other offences against the person extend from the relatively minor assault and battery case to the causing grievous bodily harm which may only just fall short of being homicide.

(ii) *Crimes against property.*—In this category the essence of the crime is the wrongful taking of someone else's property or "theft", as the layman would call it. Larceny, to use the lawyer's term, is defined by the Larceny Act 1916 in this way—"a person steals who, without the consent of the owner, fraudulently and without a claim of right made in good faith takes and carries away anything capable of being stolen, with intent, at the time of such taking, permanently to deprive the owner thereof". From this involved definition it will be seen that the crime of larceny does not cover all that the layman would mean by theft, and so there are a number of kindred offences in criminal law to meet this difficulty. Hence there is an offence of obtaining by false pretences, another of embezzlement, then fraudulent conversion, falsification of accounts, receiving stolen goods, and so on. Similarly where the theft involves entering someone else's property this may lead to a charge of burglary (breaking into or out of a dwelling house between 9 p.m. and 6 a.m. intending to commit or having committed a felony therein) or it may be housebreaking or, in the appropriate circumstances, it may be robbery. It will readily be grasped that there is nothing simple about this aspect of the criminal law.

(iii) *Crimes against public rights.*—In this category falls treason, the most serious of all crimes, although in recent years most cases have been brought as breaches of the Official Secrets Acts. Lesser offences which are not frequently in the news are sedition, unlawful assembly, riot and causing an affray; and, as rather strange bed-fellows, bigamy and criminal libel.

The categories and the crimes mentioned above are meant to be illustrative and certainly not exhaustive so from what little has been said it must be obvious that criminal law as an aspect of public law warrants a very large treatment to itself. This book however is not the place for such a treatment although the student must keep in mind that a full understanding of public law would involve a full study of criminal law. For the purpose of this book public law is looked at entirely from the civil law standpoint, only again touching on criminal law aspects in the cases affecting the liberties of the subject.

(b) Constitutional and administrative law

Public law on the civil law side tends to consist in those subjects which fall within the fields of constitutional and administrative law. This involves a study of the organs of government: for example, the role of the Monarch, Parliament, the courts, the civil service and local government—and continues into the practical activities of these various organs. Constitutional law limits itself to the origins, development and current role of all the organs of government, whilst administrative law is concerned with the grounds on which and the methods by which the courts may hold in check the various organs of government when their powers are challenged. Both fields of law are substantial and administrative law in particular is complex; in this book, which is an introduction to the subject, little more can be done than to emphasise the principles which form the basis of the system. All the main topics are dealt with in the course of this book although a lay-out has been used which it is hoped will bring home to the student the highly practical nature of the subject. The aim is to show that Parliament and its delegated bodies are all the time creating new law; so too in a quite different way are the judges; and so too are the administrative bodies which are the new development in English law. To curb any excess of law-making power it is necessary to see what powers the courts exercise in this matter. What remedies can they give? Under what conditions? Is the control effective? And then having considered all these factors the most important final topic remains how far does the man in the street retain his liberty in all this? Is he a free man? If not, in what ways are his liberties curtailed? And with what justification?

These are the civil law matters which affect public law as a subject of study.

5 THE LEGAL PROFESSION

In England the legal profession is divided into two classes known as barristers and solicitors. The term "lawyer" is appropriate to either class, and to become a lawyer one has to undergo special training and pass a number of examinations before the governing bodies of the professions will allow the would-be lawyer to enter. In addition to the rules which control entry to the professions the professional conduct of members is also rigorously supervised. This is done to ensure that when a member of the public finds it necessary to consult a lawyer he can have full confidence in the integrity of the lawyer he employs.

At the present time the two classes of lawyer are kept completely apart; they carry out quite different functions, they undergo different training and they have different governing bodies. In consequence each class will be treated independently and finally brief consideration will be given to the arguments for and against having one legal profession, or " fusion" as it has come to be called.

(a) Barristers

(i) *General.*—A barrister, formally a barrister-at-law, is so called because when he satisfies all the requirements for entry to the profession, he is said to be "called to the Bar". The Bar in question being the bar of the court. Another word used to describe barristers is "counsel". Thus one talks of "counsel for the prosecution" or "counsel for the defence" and in court the judge always refers to the advocates as "counsel". The word emphasises the role of the barrister in court; he is there to give "counsel", or advice, to the court so that the court may arrive at a proper decision. A barrister is not in court to win at all costs; his duty is to his client and to the court to give the best "counsel" he can in the circumstances of the case.

(ii) *Senior and junior counsel.*—All the 2,000 barristers who are in practice are either junior counsel or Queen's Counsel. The majority will be junior counsel because only a select few are specially appointed by the Queen, through the Lord Chancellor's recommendation, to be Queen's Counsel. Some twenty receive the honour each year and altogether at any one time there will only be some 200 "Q.C.'s" in practice. In order to achieve this distinction the Barrister must be able to show that he has had at least ten years' experience and that he has established a successful practice as a junior counsel. One odd feature of the distinction is that one has to apply to the Lord Chancellor for it. The reason for this is that there are special rules of professional conduct which affect a Q.C. once appointed, for example, he may not appear in a case unless he is accompanied by at least one junior counsel, and there are certain kinds of routine legal work which he must give up on becoming a Q.C. The result of this is that becoming a Q.C. is something of a speculation and not all who achieve the honour find that it turns out to their advantage; hence the reason why application to the Lord Chancellor is necessary.

All barristers who are in practice and are not Q.C.'s are therefore junior counsel. Hence one can be nearing retiring age and still be "junior" counsel; and, even more paradoxically, a well-known and very successful junior counsel may be financially and in status very much better off than a great many Queen's Counsel. Becoming a Queen's Counsel is known as "taking silk" because thereafter a silk lined gown and hood is worn, and another term which is used of a Queen's Counsel is that of "leader". A junior counsel would, in speaking of a case in which he appeared with a Q.C. talk of having X as "leader".

(iii) *The duties of a barrister.*—The work which a barrister will do is not easy to state with assurance because of the variety of legal matters with which he may be concerned. The most typical barrister is the specialist advocate. The man who can be seen in court prosecuting or defending in a criminal case, or pleading for the plaintiff or the defendant in a civil case. He wears wig and gown always, and he carries on the age-old task of presenting his client's case to the court. He is essentially an advocate, trained and experienced in the rules of the court and so able to do the pleading for the client which the client is not able to do for himself. Much criticism has been directed at the role of the barrister. He is "paid to tell lies" it is said. This shows a complete misunderstanding of the barrister's position. The barrister does not "tell lies", his professional duty to the court would prevent this. His task is to present his client's case to the court and in doing so he acts entirely on the client's instructions. If his client is telling lies that is not for the barrister but for the court to say. The barrister may warn and advise his client but fundamentally he must present the case on the basis of his instructions; if the barrister were left to choose to defend only those persons he himself believed to be innocent the vast majority of accused persons would find it difficult, if not impossible, to obtain the services of a barrister. The barrister is not expressing his own personal views to the court, he is presenting his client's explanation and defence; the barrister's personal views are never invited and, it is safe to say, should never be expressed. The tactics which the barrister employs in attacking prosecution witnesses and picking holes in the prosecution case can be justified on the basis that the full onus of proof is on the prosecution, and he is therefore quite properly entitled to point to weakness in that case.

The typical barrister's work then is advocacy in the courts but here again there is a great deal of difference between the defence of an accused person in a criminal trial and say the complex argument in an involved case about liability for income tax or dealing with the re-arrangement of the financial structure of a company. A really successful barrister will therefore be accustomed to appearing before all sorts of courts and enquiries in all sorts of cases, civil and criminal, prosecuting or defending, or acting for the plaintiff or for the defendant.

On the other hand it would be a mistake to think of the barrister only as an advocate since some very successful barristers hardly ever appear in court. The point is that some barristers will specialise in the different branches of law; one will become an expert on town and country planning, another on tax law and another on conveyancing. In the result such barristers will spend most of their time preparing documents, giving written advice, even perhaps writing books, and very little (if any) of their time will be spent on advocacy. Even those barristers who are specialists in advocacy must spend a considerable proportion of their time on paper work. They have to study their brief, which is the case as prepared by the solicitor instructing the barrister and then give advice as to the witnesses who are to be called and also request further information to help in preparing the case for presentation in court. In a civil case the whole of the process which leads to trial involves the use of documents known as pleadings (see chapter 3. The procedure of the court—Civil) and all of these must be prepared by the barrister. In addition a solicitor having a particular query will often prepare a case for a barrister's "opinion" and this too involves the barrister in having to prepare a written reply to the questions asked. So it is somewhat misleading to see a barrister only as performing in court; much will depend on the particular barrister.

(iv) *The barrister's independence.*—One factor which stands out in the work of the barrister is the way in which he is dependent upon the solicitor for his instructions. The barrister by the rules of his profession is not permitted to meet the public direct; his services can only be obtained through a solicitor. The result of this isolation is seen again in that barristers do not spend much time in the presence of the client or of witnesses; often they meet only a few moments before the case begins and in general this state of affairs helps to preserve the barrister's objectivity. The solicitor does all the preparation, taking the statements of the client and the witnesses, seeing that they are at court when required and furnishing the barrister with all the evidence which he has asked for. Thus to the barrister all cases are as one; today he prosecutes, and tomorrow he defends. It matters not to the professional advocate. He gives of the best of his skill to each case and cultivates an aura of objectivity which enables him to be fearless and independent yet courteous to the court and ever mindful of his over-riding duty to his client. No-one who has seen barristers at work in the courts will have failed to notice the air of civilised controversy in which the case is conducted. It is very far removed from the Perry Mason approach.

Barristers are not allowed to form partnerships but although working independently they do share chambers and also, which in practice is more important, they often share a clerk, through whom their business is negotiated. Solicitors always have to contact the barrister's clerk in order to obtain the barrister's services, and it is with the clerk that the barrister's fee is agreed. The brief is marked with this fee together with a fee for the clerk. The strangest feature of this situation is that the barrister is not able to sue for his fees: this is because of the ancient fiction that a barrister's services are gratuitous and that his fee is really a gift! The gown which the barrister wears has, as a standard feature, a special pocket in which the grateful client is expected to slip his "gift". This is the theory only and in practice it never happens!

(v) *Liability for negligence.*—It has long been the rule that barristers cannot be sued for negligence, the law maintaining the presumption that as a result of his training and experience a barrister will not fail in his duty to his client and to the court. This old rule has recently been challenged in the courts in the case of *Rondel* v. *Worsley* (1967) but the Court of Appeal (Civil Division) upheld the immunity of the barrister. The rule is now to be considered by the House of Lords in a further appeal the result of which will be of great consequence to the legal profession. Another rule connected with this immunity in negligence is that where a solicitor obtains and acts on the advice of a barrister then he, in turn, cannot successfully be sued for negligence.

(vi) *The assize circuit.*—Barristers, once qualified to practise, must at once begin to specialise. Some go to the Chancery Bar, some to the Common Law Bar and others to the Parliamentary Bar; those who intend to practise on one of the seven assize circuits must arrange to join the circuit of their choice. Once he has made a selection the barrister must substantially restrict his activities to the circuit in question. Naturally most barristers practise in London but it is possible to find members of the Bar in most large cities in this country.

(vii) *Becoming a barrister.*—The steps by which a would-be barrister obtains the qualification and is able to set up in practice are quite straightforward. Assuming that the student has a reasonable educational background and has the requisite "O" and "A" level passes he (or she) must arrange to register with one of the four Inns of Court. These are Gray's Inn, Lincoln's Inn, Middle Temple and Inner Temple. Once registered the student must over a three-year period attend his Inn to eat each term a prescribed number of dinners and also to take and pass the necessary legal examinations set by the Council for Legal Education. The reason for the apparently strange requirement concerning the eating of dinners is the desire to ensure that all students become steeped in the atmosphere of the legal world. On completion of the three year period he is "called to the Bar" and is entitled to call himself a barrister-at-law. If now the barrister intends to practise he must spend a further year understudying the work of a junior counsel. This year is known as "pupillage" and the intention is that the young barrister will in effect begin to learn his trade by spending all his time for one year shadowing a successful barrister actually in practice. This year completed the barrister is able to begin to practise on his own account. An interesting development in the field of training barristers has been the tremendous number of overseas students who have come to England to obtain the barrister's qualification. At one time 75 per cent of students qualifying as barristers were from overseas.

(viii) *The discipline of the Bar.*—The Inn of Court with which the student originally registered and which later "called" him remains responsible for his professional conduct all the time that he continues in practice. Each Inn has its own governing body known as benchers who are its senior members and the benchers have considerable powers to discipline the barristers of that Inn. They may censure, suspend and in the last resort disbar a barrister whose professional conduct falls short of the standard expected by the profession. Fortunately such drastic action is only very rarely called for.

(ix) *The barrister's career.*—The prospects of the barrister depend on a number of factors over which he himself has limited control. His greatest problem is that he cannot obtain work from the public direct; he must always be instructed by a solicitor. No matter how talented he may be, he will starve unless he is known to solicitors, and it is for this reason that a clerk is so valuable, as also the contacts which the young barrister will have made through his "pupillage". Even so, for many barristers Lady Luck plays a vital part; a good performance noted by a very busy solicitor may well be the turning point of a career. Once established the barrister can with increasing success have an eye to becoming a Q.C. and to his prospects of achieving office as a Recorder and ultimately of elevation to the judicial bench.

(b) Solicitors

(i) *General.*—The younger branch of the profession differs from the elder in a number of significant ways, but most especially in that whereas the barrister never meets the public direct, the solicitor is always available to the public. The solicitor can display his name plate and then deal with the business of any member of the public who cares to consult him on any matter. Altogether there are some 22,000 solicitors in practice in England and Wales although not all of these are in private practice. A considerable number of solicitors (and barristers too) are employed in the civil service, in local authorities, in public corporations, in the academic world, and in industry but most of what will now be said about solicitors refers particularly to those who are engaged in private practice.

(ii) *The solicitor's work.*—Solicitors spend their time dealing with practical matters in all fields of law. Whatever problems beset the layman these are the problems which will find their way on to the solicitor's desk. The buying and selling or renting of property and all the complex arrangements with regard to raising the purchase money, arranging the details for moving out of the one house and into the other, ensuring by the study and preparation of the necessary documents that a good title in law is given and obtained, these matters are almost always conducted by solicitors. This procedure known as conveyancing is the main activity of most solicitors and they are paid a fee depending on the value of the property and the type of title investigation called for. On a sale of a house for £3,000 on the registered land scale the buyer and the seller will each pay his solicitor a fee of £35. If the unregistered land scale applies the fee will be £52. 10. od. On a £4,000 sale the fees will be either £40 or £60. In addition if the buyer is having a mortgage to assist him in finding the purchase price the solicitor will, because of the extra work involved, receive a further fee depending on the size of the mortgage. In return for the fee he receives the solicitor guarantees his client that he will account for the full purchase price to the vendor if he is selling, or that the purchaser is getting a good legal title to the property if he is buying. His services are thus a form of insurance to the layman. Another task of the solicitor is the drawing up of legal documents such as contracts, partnership agreements, wills and trust deeds. The mention of wills points the way to the large amount of probate work done by solicitors in the winding up of the estates of deceased persons. In another field of law many solicitors engage in litigation on behalf of their clients.

(iii) *The solicitor and the court.*—Although there is only a limited right for a solicitor to himself act as advocate in court, he being restricted generally to appearing in the magistrates' court or the County Court; nonetheless the preparation of all cases for trial, whether civil or criminal and at all levels must, save where the person represents himself, be done by a solicitor. Where he has no right of audience the solicitor will instruct the barrister who will actually appear in court. This means that anybody who wishes to obtain a High Court decision, whether it be by way of a petition for divorce or by an action for money owing on a debt or arising from a breach of contract, in virtually all such cases a solicitor will be consulted and he will be required to handle all the stages of the case except the actual court hearing. These illustrations of the work of the solicitor, conveyancing, probate and litigation, are intended to be typical and not in any way exhaustive, since the thousands of ways in which law can affect the individual means that there is no end to the matters on which a solicitor may be consulted.

(iv) *The solicitor in practice.*—Solicitors are permitted to form partnerships and this they frequently do. The main advantages are the opportunity which this gives to the solicitors to specialise in the fields of law of their choice and also the opportunity of ready access to another qualified man when a second opinion is needed. Some of the most important firms of solicitors in London consist of twenty or more partners, but in the country as a whole the average firm has probably three partners. Even so there are a great many one-man practices. Once qualified a solicitor is required to take out each year a practising certificate and this involves the payment of £11 to the Law Society, the governing body of the profession, and a payment of, at present, £8 to the contribution fund. This fund is maintained to reimburse any client who suffers financial loss as a result of professional misconduct by a solicitor. In addition, and unlike the barrister, a solicitor can be sued for professional negligence by a client and such actions are by no means uncommon. Where however the solicitor is acting on the advice of a barrister he is protected against an action in negligence. Most of the charges which solicitors make are laid down under statutory powers and they are therefore entitled to sue for their fees: in this they differ from barristers who cannot sue for their fees.

The name "solicitor" is connected with the fact that the person concerned "solicited" the services of a barrister to plead a case in court. The early name for a solicitor was "attorney". The old role is seen plainly in the way the modern solicitor still prepares the "brief" which contains the instructions for the barrister to plead the case in court.

(v) *Becoming a solicitor.*—The course which a would-be solicitor must follow in order to qualify is quite different from that taken by the would-be barrister. Once he (or she) has the required "O" and "A" level passes the student must find a practising solictor who is prepared to take him as an articled clerk. This procedure means that for the required period of time the articled clerk must be prepared to spend his time in his principal's office learning by observation the work of a solicitor. The length of time in question depends on the academic qualifications of the student: for a law graduate the period is two and a half years, for any other Graduate three years, with certain "A" level passes four years and with minimum qualifications five years. Besides the requirement of articles, the practical training, the student must pass a succession of law examinations and in order to do so he is expected to attend law school prior to the examinations. On successfully passing the examinations and completing articles the student is formally "admitted" as a solicitor by the Master of the Rolls. Thereafter he is entitled to take out a practising certificate and put up his name-plate.

(vi) *The discipline of the profession.*—The solicitors' branch of the profession is controlled by the Law Society which is by Statute responsible for the discipline of all solicitors. For serious professional misconduct it is possible for a solicitor to be censured, fined, or suspended, or in the last resort ordered to have his name struck off the rolls of the court. This latter course is necessary because the solicitor on admission is made an officer of the Supreme Court of Judicature. One most important rule which solicitors must observe is that they must keep the money belonging to their clients in an account separate from their own money. A failure to do this will lose the solicitor his right to practise.

(vii) *The career of a solicitor.*—The solicitor's prospects, once he is admitted, are good. There has been for several years a serious shortage of solicitors and this has meant that a newly qualified solicitor can command a very substantial four-figure salary and with experience he can carve out a career for himself whether in private practice or in the public service which will assure him of a good standard of living.

(viii) *Barristers and solicitors.*—It will be seen from what has been said that the layman's view of the barrister as a superior lawyer is quite inaccurate. This view seems to have caught on because of a combination of factors: the isolation of the barrister from the public: his exalted appearance in wig and gown in court: the undue esteem of the age for specialisation: and the small numbers of the profession. In fact it is generally agreed that it is more difficult to qualify as a solicitor than to be called to the Bar: on the other hand, once qualified, it is more difficult to become a successful barrister for the reasons explained above. Once successful the barrister has much more glamorous prospects than the solicitor, since in time he may become a Queen's Counsel and later be offered a judgeship. The right of audience before the superior courts is limited to barristers and in the result all the judges throughout the court structure are chosen from the ranks of practising barristers.

(c) **Fusion of the legal profession**

The question is often asked whether or not there is any need for the legal profession to be divided. The critics suggest that the reason for the division is a matter of history and that the time has come to unite the two branches. If this were done, the critics allege, the cost of litigation would be reduced, matters would be handled with greater efficiency and selection for judgeship would be from a wider field of talent. Moreover it is argued, many countries do have a united legal profession and their legal systems operate effectively.

Those people who prefer the present arrangement rebut these arguments in this way. First of all it is not necessarily true that such a system will lower costs. It might seem that instead of employing a solicitor and a barrister as at present that in future the one lawyer will carry the case through alone. If one lawyer does take the case will he not, in practice, require the equivalent of the two fees? But, more important, it seems most unlikely that many of the persons who are at present solicitors will either be capable of advocacy or will wish to engage in it. Besides, how can they be available to their clients in their offices if they are also to spend their time in court? In other words the supporters of the *status quo* argue that the present system operates well and the suggested change would not make for improvement or result in any real saving in costs. What financial saving there is will be more than made up for by the lowering of advocacy standards resulting from the weakening of the present specialisation. Whereas at present advocates in the superior courts are all specialists in the field, under a fused system every lawyer however limited his experience would be able to appear in any court in any type of case. People who hold this view would also argue that in those countries which nominally have fusion there is in practice a division between the specialist advocates and non-advocates. This means that if a client goes to the office of a particular advocate he will almost certainly be seen by a non-advocate lawyer who will prepare the case before handing it at its final vital stage to the advocate—and this is so like the barrister/solicitor relationship in this country that no change is necessary.

6   LEGAL AID AND ADVICE

(a) Growth and development

It is obvious that there is no point in having a perfect system of justice administered by brilliant judges unless everyone in the State can afford the cost of using the courts. For a long time in this country the cynical maxim that "Justice is open to all like the Ritz Hotel" was too near the truth for comfort. The courts have always been open to all, but what consolation would this be to a person who felt he had a valid claim, or equally a good defence to a claim, and yet had not the money to contemplate bringing or defending the action? How much more serious when the matter was a criminal charge and the prosecution would be handled by a lawyer?

It was in the criminal law field that the social conscience first felt the need for legal representation for an accused person although for a long time it was left to public spirited members of the legal profession to provide the service on a more or less voluntary basis. A relic of this history is the dock brief system under which any accused person at his trial may, provided he can produce £2 4s. 6d. in cash, call on the services of any barrister present in court. In view of the hasty preparations involved in so important a matter it is as well that the dock brief is nearly obsolete. Gradually improvements were made by Acts of Parliament and it has become acknowledged that the State ought to provide legal representation in criminal cases for accused persons. The details of the present position will be considered below.

In civil law matters, however, no such provision was thought to be necessary and such assistance as was furnished was provided under the Poor Persons Procedure system and this required the services of lawyers free of charge. This failure to provide even an advice service was brought to a head by the 1939–1945 War when each of the three Services found it necessary to establish an advisory body for serving members of the forces and the Law Society did likewise for the civilian population. A committee under Lord Rushcliffe was set up in 1944 and it reported in 1945 recommending the provision on a financial means test basis of state financed legal aid and advice. These recommendations were given effect by Parliament in the Legal Aid and Advice Act 1949 and the provisions of this Act as gradually implemented and as amended in 1960 and 1964 are still in force. Naturally the detailed financial content has been brought into line with changes in the value of money but the basic conception remains unaltered. The Act now applies to all the civil courts and the only type of case in which legal aid is not yet available is for actions before tribunals and inquiries.

(b) Legal aid in criminal cases

As has been said it is now the case that free legal aid is available to accused persons when charged with the more serious criminal offences and for appeals. The legislation affecting the situation is complex and different rules apply to different courts. The principal Act is the Poor Prisoners Defence Act 1930 but this has been much amended particularly by the Legal Aid and Advice Act 1949.

The magistrates are able to grant a legal aid certificate on a summary trial or when holding a preliminary enquiry (these terms will be explained in chapter 3). Such a certificate entitles the accused to have a solicitor to represent him and in the case of a murder charge, a solicitor and a barrister. For a trial at quarter sessions or assizes the court can grant a defence certificate and this also will entitle the accused to representation by solicitor and barrister. Where there is an Appeal in a criminal case it is very possible that the Appeal Court will grant legal aid in the form of representation by a barrister.

There is no independent examination into the accused's means in these cases, and the rather haphazard basis on which legal aid is given has been much criticised. A committee under the chairmanship of Mr. Justice Widgery reported in 1965/1966 in favour of the courts being given power to order the accused to make a contribution towards the cost of legal aid. Since the general principle is that in cases of doubt assistance should be given to the accused and since also there is no half-way house, the accused either getting free legal aid or none at all, there is no doubt that the present system is not as sound as that used in civil cases.

(c) Legal aid in civil cases

In civil cases the position is governed by the Legal Aid and Advice Act 1949 as amended in 1960 and 1964. Under its provisions any person who wishes to bring an action, whether for example a petition for divorce or a claim for damages for some loss which he has suffered, must formally apply in writing to a local legal aid committee. Local committees consist of solicitors and barristers and are established throughout the country. These local committees are answerable to twelve area committees and these in turn must answer to the Law Society which is the body charged under the 1949

Act with the responsibility for organising, with the Lord Chancellor's approval, the civil legal aid scheme on a national basis.

(i) *The local committee.*—The task of the local committee is to consider the applicant's claim or defence to determine whether or not his application reveals reasonable grounds for pursuing the case. This decision is made on the practical basis of the lawyer's view of what are reasonable grounds. No legal aid is available for claims based on libel, slander, breach of promise of marriage, seduction or enticement since these are highly personal actions and it is not felt that they need to fall within a scheme of State assisted actions. If the local committee refuses the application, appeal is to the area committee and in a case where legal aid is sought for an appeal to the Court of Appeal or the House of Lords the application must be decided by the area committee. An appeal against refusal lies to the Court of Appeal.

(ii) *The financial question.*—Assuming that the local committee are satisfied that the applicant's case warrants legal aid, the second stage in the procedure is for the Ministry of Social Security (the former National Assistance Board) to carry out an investigation into the financial resources of the applicant. Depending on this investigation will be the actual amount of assistance, if any, which the applicant will get. Provision extends from no legal aid at all to completely free legal aid with, in between, provision for partial legal aid subject to a maximum contribution from the applicant. The means test carried out by the Ministry of Social Security is based on two major factors, "disposable income" and "disposable capital". A person's "disposable income" is his gross annual income less, for example, tax, rent or mortgage payments, and deductions for maintenance of dependants, and similarly a person's "disposable capital" allows deductions from gross capital of, for example, the value of a house in which the applicant lives (unless the value, after deducting a mortgage exceeds £3,000) and the applicant's furniture. The actual details are to be found in the Legal Aid (Assessment of Resources) Regulations, made under the authority of the 1949 Act. The present figures are that if disposable income is under £350 and disposable capital under £125 then there will be free legal aid: at the other extreme, if disposable income is more than £700 or disposable capital more than £500 then there will be no legal aid available. In between these extremes some legal aid will be given subject to a stipulated contribution payable by instalments by the applicant. This contribution will be the maximum amount that the applicant will have to pay towards his own costs if he loses the case. He thus has two major advantages; he knows from the beginning exactly what his maximum commitment is and he can meet that commitment by instalments.

(iii) *General*.—The legal aid scheme now applies to all the civil courts, having since 1949 been gradually introduced so as to spread the cost. The only proceedings for which such aid is not available is at hearings before administrative tribunals and inquiries, and it is hoped that in due course these too will be covered by the system.

One development worthy of note has been brought about by the Legal Aid Act 1964 under which where a person who is not legally aided wins his case against a legally aided opponent the successful party may, in the discretion of the court, recover all or part of his costs out of the legal aid fund

The legal aid fund is supported by Treasury grant and by the contributions of persons assisted and costs recovered from opponents. The cost to the State this year is estimated at £6 million and the annual increase is working out on average to be £1 million.

Solicitors and barristers receive 90 per cent of their normal costs in legal aid cases. Some object to this enforced subsidy of the scheme but others take the view that at least there are no bad debts and there is no difficulty with collection. Certainly it must be true that the scheme brings a lot of work to lawyers which they would not otherwise have.

(d) Legal advice

Under the provisions of the 1949 Act dealing with legal advice, arrangements have been made whereby for a nominal payment of 2s. 6d. a solicitor can be consulted. The solicitor is paid a fee out of the legal aid fund of £1 for a thirty-minute interview. The means test which is applied to the applicant is rather more stringent for legal advice than for legal aid. If the applicant has not more than £125 disposable capital and not more than £390 disposable income he will get his legal advice for nothing.

In addition to the Legal Aid and Advice Act provisions the Law Society are also operating a scheme whereby anyone, without any means test, can consult a solicitor for a fee of £1 for a half-hour interview.

7 THE SOURCES OF ENGLISH LAW

The word "sources" in this context can be regarded as the equivalent of the word "origins". In every branch of law it is possible to trace back any principle of law to its origin or source. Sometimes the source in question will be a section of an Act of Parliament, sometimes it will be a principle derived from the decision in a particular case, occasionally it may be the result of some age-old custom or the judicially accepted view of a leading text-book writer. In all these instances an attempt is made to trace back the law as it exists to its origin wherever that may be. This is quite different from studying what the law is. One can know what the law is and yet have little or no idea of the authority for that law. In the introduction to this chapter when surveying the topics which would be covered, three actual situations were put forward for consideration in the attempt to explain the practical implications of the phrase "the sources of English law". The first question asked was "where is the source of law which stipulates that a car driver must not exceed 70 miles per hour?" The answer to that question is Statutory Instrument 1966/639 being the 70 miles per hour (Temporary Speed Limit) (England) (No. 2) Order 1966. The second question asked was "where is the source of law which requires a driver to be insured against certain risks?" The answer to that question is section 201 of the Road Traffic Act 1960. The third question asked was "where is the source of law which requires the driver of a motor vehicle to pay compensation to a pedestrian injured by his negligent driving?" The answer to this question is not as straightforward as the other answers because here the answer is that there are very many actual cases which have been reported in which judges have held such drivers responsible for the tort of negligence. This means that in the first two instances the source of the law in question is legislation, whereas in the third instance the source of the law is case law.

The two major and the two minor sources of law will now be considered in turn:
legislation, case law, custom, books of authority.

(a) Legislation

At the present time legislation is much the most important source of new law. By legislation is meant Acts of Parliament and such Acts openly create new law. Every Act of Parliament in one way or another changes the law and since Parliament is supreme every one must accept and abide by these Acts when once they have passed through the proper process and become law. There is no power in the State which can overrule an Act of Parliament; even the judiciary has no power to refuse to apply an Act. The task of the judiciary is to "interpret" the words used in the Act in cases which come before them.

In addition to the creation of new law by Acts of Parliament the pressure of business is such that for many years Parliament has been passing on (or delegating) its power to make law to certain other bodies. Naturally this power is given subject to very clear conditions and for very limited purposes but such new law when properly made is called delegated legislation and takes effect just like an Act of Parliament. The best examples of delegated legislation are:

(a) a power given to a Minister of the Crown through his department to make detailed rules and regulations to implement a policy which Parliament has authorised in outline. Such rules and regulations when formally issued in accordance with the Act are known as Statutory Instruments.

(b) Local authorities have been given power to make by-laws which when approved will operate as law in their locality, and

(c) similarly public corporations have been given power to make by-laws for their own limited purposes. The British Railways Board, for example, have made many by-laws to assist in the management of the Railways.

The total bulk of legislation and delegated legislation is enormous but it is to this source that the lawyer will frequently have to turn to discover the authority for the proposition which he knows to exist in law. The part played by Parliament in the making of law will be explained in chapter 2 and it will only be when the student has completed a study of that chapter that he will have a full appreciation of legislation as a source of English law.

(b) Case Law

(i) *Importance.*—Chaucer's Serjeant at Law in the Prologue to "The Canterbury Tales" is portrayed as being an outstanding lawyer of his day (c. 1380) because he knew all the leading cases and judgments which had taken place since the reign of William the Conqueror. So today it would also be true that an outstanding lawyer would need to be well-versed in leading cases and judgments, although not those extending quite so far back as Chaucer's day!

For obvious reasons great respect is paid to the decisions of judges in the cases which have come before them. For several centuries these decisions in cases of any consequence have been reported and so the reasoning of the judge or judges has been made available to posterity. One of the characteristics of English law is that certain branches of the law, in particular contract and tort, have been gradually built up almost entirely as the result of these decided cases. The principles which have come to be acknowledged are all traceable to actual cases, and in that sense even at the present time a decision in a new case based in contract or tort may have some bearing on the existing principles. It is thus easy to understand why cases are so important.

Every time a judge gives judgment he is in a sense making law. In chapter 3 a fuller study will be made of the contribution made by the courts in this process of making law. At this stage the emphasis is on case law as a source of public law. Perhaps therefore the easiest approach is to take a leading case in this branch of law and consider its implications.

A good example is the *Attorney-General* v. *De Keyser's Royal Hotel Ltd.* (1920). In this case the Crown, *i.e.* the Government, having failed to obtain by agreement a letting of hotel premises for military purposes during the First World War, compulsorily took possession of the hotel. On a claim by the owners for compensation the Crown sought to escape liability on the grounds that the seizure took place under the royal prerogative in time of emergency. The House of Lords refused to accept this argument holding that the statutory Defence of the Realm Acts applied and these entitled the owners to compensation. The court held that where there is an Act of Parliament in force its provisions supersede the use of prerogative powers. The decision in this case provides a principle of public law; that where a prerogative power and a statutory provision conflict the statutory provision shall prevail. This principle, derived as it is from a case, is just as effective as if a section of an Act of Parliament had actually enacted the principle.

The cumulative effect of all the cases which have been decided in the past and of all the cases which are currently being decided, makes case law a vitally significant source of public law. This will be seen to be so when in chapter 6 a survey is made of the liberties of the individual. Many of the principles of law about police powers of arrest or about the right of public meeting, to take two examples, are based on decided cases and not on Acts of Parliament at all.

(ii) *Judicial precedent.*—As might be expected greater stress is laid on the decisions of the appeal courts than on those of first instance. This natural respect has developed into a rigid system which has surrendered flexibility and which has led to the creation of what is known as the doctrine of judicial precedent, *i.e.* decisions of judges in former cases. Under this doctrine a decision of the House of Lords is "binding" on all the lower courts in the structure. In the same way a decision of the Court of Appeal will bind all the courts lower than itself. As between judges of equal standing, say High Court judges, although their judgments are not binding on each other they are said to be "persuasive". The doctrine, it can be said, follows through the hierarchy of the courts which will be fully explained in chapter 3.

On the other hand there have been recent signs that the courts have recognised that the doctrine can be too rigidly applied. In particular the House of Lords announced through the Lord Chancellor in 1966 that it will not regard itself for the future as necessarily bound by its former decisions. Whilst no-one would wish to see the general principle of so valid a doctrine completely destroyed it is certainly desirable that changes in social outlook and manners should be recognised in the courts. The principle on which the House of Lords decided a case in 1750 or 1850 may clearly have little relevance today. Too often in the past judges have had to say "I am bound to decide this case in favour of the defendant because of the decision in the case of X *v.* Y. I do so with regret but in view of the precedent I have no alternative." The only other way in which a judge can escape from a binding precedent is for him to "distinguish" it from the facts of the case before him. Such distinguishing has sometimes sprung from a desire to avoid following the precedent and has almost resulted in sophistry.

Strictly a judge of a lower court must "follow" the principle laid down in a case by a higher court if the precedent is in point. If it is not in point then the judge can "distinguish" it from the present case. It is not difficult to understand the problem faced by a judge when counsel are able to present him with many precedents, some of which would seem to favour the plaintiff's argument whilst the others seem to favour the defendant. When such a judge gives his judgment he will explain his reasoning in relation to the principles of law and the precedents involved and in this sense his judgment is making law. Whatever he decides is a ruling of the law on the particular facts in this case. It is only if and when that ruling is considered by a higher court that that statement of the law will either be approved or questioned or disapproved.

No two cases are likely to be exactly the same in every particular. This means that however close a precedent may seem to be to the facts of a case there may be a factor in the new situation which did not occur in the former and it may be that because of this factor the precedent will be held not to be in point.

(iii) *The decision.*—Every case decision can be analysed into two parts: the *ratio decidendi*, by which is meant "the reason for the decision", and *obiter dicta*, "things said by the way". It is the *ratio decidendi* of a precedent which is the vital factor to a judge considering

it: he has to pick out of the judgment the crucial reasoning of the
court which led it to make the decision it did. This is normally
the application of some principle of law to the facts of the case.
Difficulties become apparent when several principles of law appear
to be relevant: this means that sometimes there is more than one
ratio (*rationes*) for the decision. It is not uncommon for counsel to
argue over what is the exact *ratio decidendi* of a precedent. These
are the factors which make a judge's task difficult in deciding which
precedents he must follow in a case before him. The *obiter dicta* are
the explanations and comments which a judge makes in the course
of giving judgment but which are not vitally relevant to the actual
decision in the case.

To take an example: if a judge is hearing a factory accident case
he will probably be concerned with whether or not the employer
had provided a safe system of work; in deciding he will not only
hear the evidence of the employer, the employee and their respective
witnesses but he will also need to consider the relevant precedents
which have dealt with safe systems of work. The actual decision he
gives will either be that the plaintiff succeeds, or the defendant
succeeds, but he must then explain fully why it is that in law he feels
driven to this conclusion. The detailed reasoning on this point is
the *ratio decidendi*. If, however, in the course of his judgment the
judge discusses alternative systems of work, which might or might not
be "safe", then this discussion would be "*obiter dicta*" since it is not
directly relevant to the decision.

(c) Custom

(i) *Minor source of law.*—At the present time custom is not a very
prominent source of law but regard must be had to it because
English law very largely emanated from it. In any State the early
development of law derives substantially from the customs of the
people; it could hardly be otherwise. As time passes the customs
are either restated in Acts of Parliament or they are pleaded and
given effect in actual cases so developing into case law. The result
is that at this late stage in the development of English law, virtually
all customs have been so dealt with, and it is very unusual for a plea
of custom to be put forward in a case today.

(ii) *Requirements.*—Nonetheless custom is a source of law and
where the circumstances satisfy the legal requirements the plea
will be upheld in the courts. These legal requirements can be
summarised as:

(1) the custom must have existed from time immemorial, which is fixed at 1189 A.D.—the first year of the reign of Richard I. This does not mean that the claimant must produce proof of the existence of the custom for the whole of that period. This would be impossible so the court allows a presumption that the custom in question dates back to 1189 A.D. provided that the evidence of the oldest inhabitant confirms that it has existed throughout his life-time. It is open to the other party to rebut this presumption by showing that the custom could not have existed in 1189 A.D.—because for example of the change in the value of money, *Bryant* v. *Foot* (1868) (an alleged customary fee of 13s. on the celebration of a marriage would have been a totally unreasonable amount in 1189 A.D.), or because the custom specifically dates from a later event, *Simpson* v. *Wells* (1872) (where the event in question arose following a Statute passed in the fourteenth century).

(2) the custom must be certain in its application as to the subject matter and the persons benefited.

(3) the custom must have existed continuously and without objection. The legal expression is *"nec vi, nec clam, nec precario"*, which means that the custom has not been exercised by force, secretly or with permission. Hence if what is claimed as a custom is done under the grant of a licence the claim of custom will not be upheld, *Mills* v. *Colchester Corporation* (1867) (the corporation granted licences to fish their oyster fishery— there could thus not be a custom to require a licence to be granted).

A leading case in which a claim of custom was upheld was *Mercer* v. *Denne* (1905). In this case fishermen of Walmer, Kent, successfully claimed a right by custom to dry their nets on a particular piece of private ground.

A recent case in which a claim of custom for certain villagers to collect sea coal from the foreshore near Hartlepool, County Durham, was made but failed, was *Beckett, Ltd.* v. *Lyons* (1966). It was held by the Court of Appeal that the circumstances of the case did not justify the plea of custom; but it is worthy of remark that the plea had succeeded before the judge at first instance.

(d) Books of authority

(i) *Use in court.*—This is a comparatively minor source of law but it must be included since in practice lawyers spend as much time consulting the acknowledged text-books in a particular field of law as they do looking up actual precedents. This is true not only of the practising lawyer but also of the judge sitting in court, because a judge will often find that the view of a particular principle of law presented by a specialist is of real value in assisting him to shape his judgment. Even if he does not agree with the views expressed the argument will often be helpful.   This is quite natural since the writer may well have specialised in his particular field to an extent which entitles his views to great respect.

As might be expected only certain outstanding specialist works are consulted.   If a counsel wishes to quote a text-book in support of a case he may be allowed by the judge to "adopt" the argument and so include it in his presentation.   By tradition these text-books are known as somebody ON some branch of law.   For example, *Chitty on Contracts* or *Rayden on Divorce*.   A further odd aspect is that these text-books go on being edited and brought up to date long after the original author's death.   For example, Chitty is now in its 22nd Edition (1961) with Supplement (1965).   The last edition by Chitty himself was the 3rd (1841).

At one time the rule was that no living text-book writer would be regarded as an "authority" in his lifetime; it is now, however, quite common for the works of living writers to be cited in court and this willingness to consider any helpful source may extend even to articles in legal periodicals provided the author is of sufficient eminence.   In a case in 1942 the Court of Appeal made use of an article by Professor A. L. Goodhart which had been published in the Law Quarterly Review.

(ii) *Old legal works.*—Another meaning of the term books of authority is that certain old legal text-books dating back several centuries will be accepted as authoritative of the law as it was at the time that they were written.   The standing of certain of these ancient authors is considerable and their works are still cited on occasions. Three of the most widely known are—Bracton's *"De Legibus et Consuetudinibus Angliae"* (c. 1250), Coke's *"Institutes of the Laws of England"* (c. 1630) and Blackstone's *"Commentaries on the Laws of England"* (c. 1765).   A recent case which resulted in a survey of some of these old text-books was *R. v. Button* (1966), where the House of Lords had to consider the technical definition of the crime of causing an affray.   In his judgment the Lord Chancellor traced the long history of what the law has meant by an affray by referring to a very considerable number of criminal law text-books dating from earliest times right down to the present day.

Chapter 2

The Making of Law by Parliament

1 INTRODUCTION

The final section of chapter 1 explained the various sources of law which are relevant to an understanding of public law. Of these sources the two most important are legislation, the making of law by Parliament which is the subject of this chapter, and case law, the making of law in the courts which will be the subject of chapter 3.

Legislation, or an Act of Parliament, is the acknowledged method by which the representatives of the people make law. In this chapter an effort will be made to discover (1) the form which legislation takes; (2) the process which legislation undergoes from the time when it is first introduced to Parliament to the moment when it becomes effective as new law; (3) the relationship which exists between the constituent parts of Parliament, *i.e.* the Monarch, the House of Lords and the House of Commons; (4) the delegated or subordinate legislation made under the authority of Parliament; and (5) the work of the judiciary in relation to legislation.

2 THE FORM OF LEGISLATION

(a) Supremacy of Parliament

In the British system of government Parliament is the supreme body. This situation is entirely the result of history and more particularly the result of the seventeenth century struggle which saw the vital power in the State pass from the Monarch to the representatives of the people. In saying that Parliament is "supreme" the intention is to stress that in Britain there is no body superior to the institution which is called Parliament. In every State there is always some person or some organisation which can enforce its will over the individuals who make up that State. This power is often referred to as "sovereignty" or "supremacy". Hence in this country the expressions—"the sovereignty of Parliament" or "the supremacy of Parliament"—are frequently used. The expressions mean that

Parliament has the power to make itself obeyed and that there is no person or organisation in the State which can declare an Act of Parliament to be of no effect. In theory it would not matter how absurd the provisions of an Act of Parliament were they would have to be obeyed. If, for example, a statute were passed which required all females to wear trousers and all males to wear skirts one result would be that be-skirted police officers would have to bring offenders before be-skirted judges—hardly a pretty picture! Nevertheless if such a provision were contained in an Act of Parliament it would be law and it could only be over-ruled by another Act of Parliament specifically repealing the earlier provision.

This supremacy of Parliament is the theory of the matter. In practice there are certain very obvious limits on the absolute power of a Parliament. One real limit is the fact that by the logic of the doctrine no Parliament can bind a succeeding Parliament. It is legally supreme only for the duration of its own lifetime. A later Parliament can, and frequently does, repeal *i.e.* cancel, Acts of previous Parliaments.

Another limit, which is a most important one, is connected with the fact that a Parliament is supreme only for its own lifetime. The reality of this situation is that the political party which is providing the Government in power and which therefore has a majority of members in the House of Commons is inevitably anxious to retain the support of the country. If it wishes to be successful at the next general election, and this cannot be more than five years away, the legislation which it introduces will have to be pleasing to the electors. There is thus a constant restriction on a Parliament to ensure that the Acts which it passes will improve the party in power's chances of re-election in due course. Add to this factor the pressure of public opinion being constantly voiced on radio and television and in the press and it is not difficult to realise how this particular limit operates.

There is also a nice academic argument about the power of a Parliament to repeal a certain type of legislation which has granted independence to an ex-colony. The general rule, that a later Parliament can repeal legislation passed by an earlier Parliament, has already been explained; but how could this apply where the legislation had granted independence to a State? The answer would seem to be that whilst in theory Parliament could repeal the legislation, in practice no notice would be paid to such repeal. No more than if Parliament by some aberration suddenly decided to make law for a foreign state. Obviously no notice would be taken by the people of the State concerned.

(b) Bills and Acts

The actual form which legislation takes has for many centuries been documentary. This means that the decisions which Parliament takes as being desirable new law are reduced to written form. In this form the draft legislation is known as "a bill" and the various provisions are numbered and called "clauses". In bill form the draft legislation is carefully considered by way of public debate; amendments are suggested and voted upon (called a division) and after a standard procedure in both the House of Commons and the House of Lords the bill in its final form receives the Royal Assent, *i.e.* the formal approval of the Monarch. The bill then changes its name and becomes "an Act" and the numbered clauses at the same moment become "sections". Unless the Act otherwise provides it becomes law immediately it receives the Royal Assent.

As each Act is passed it is given a number and is published and made available for sale through the Stationery Office. The reference system used is, in the case of public bills, to give each Act a chapter number and to refer to it under the sessional year of the Parliament which passed it. The Tribunals and Inquiries Act 1958 which will be considered in the course of chapter 4 is formally 6 and 7, Eliz. 2 c. 66. The reference means that this particular Act was the sixty-sixth Act to be passed in the session of Parliament which took place partly in the sixth and partly in the seventh year of the reign of Queen Elizabeth the Second. A private bill in the form of a local act has the chapter number in roman numerals and a personal Act has the chapter number in italics.

Delegated legislation in the form of statutory instruments is referred to on a year and serial number basis, *e.g.* Statutory Instrument 1967 No. 165 which is Registration of Title (City of Gloucester and West Midland Boroughs) Order 1967. Illustrations of an Act and a statutory instrument will be found in Appendix A, pp. 174, 175, below.

(i) *Short Titles of Acts.*—The system of formal reference is obviously somewhat cumbersome and the practice has long been common by which each Act of Parliament is referred to by a short title. This is so universal a practice that the Acts are published under their short titles. For example:

    1967   c. 1 Law Commission Act
            c. 2 Consolidated Fund Act
            c. 3 Education Act
            c. 4 West Indies Act
            c. 5 London Government Act

(ii) *Preambles and Long Titles to Acts.*—In the early history of legislation by Parliament the measure was often preceded by a formal introduction known as the preamble. This introduction formed part of the legislation and could be referred to by the judges in their task of interpretation; however, it was never treated as having the same authority as the actual words of the enactment. The purpose of the preamble was to explain in general terms the intention of the legislation and in Tudor and Stuart times it often ran to a considerable length. At the present time this fashion has substantially departed although it is not completely obsolete: in the Welsh Language Act 1967 there is a short preamble which runs "Whereas it is proper that the Welsh language should be freely used by those who so desire and on hearing all legal proceedings . . . be it therefore enacted . . . as follows". Two examples of important Acts which, in this century, have opened with a preamble are the Parliament Act 1911 and the Statute of Westminster 1931.

In the course of the centuries the preamble came to be replaced by what has become known as the long title, although there are many examples of statutes which have both a long title and a preamble. Nowadays the long title is a standard feature of legislation and like the preambles it too is now treated as an integral part of the Act and can therefore be used by the judges if of assistance in interpretation. The word "long" is not to be taken literally since a "long title" can in practice be quite short! The following examples are taken from 1966 Acts of Parliament having a bearing on public law.

c.31 Criminal Appeal Act 1966.

"An Act to transfer the Court of Criminal Appeal's jurisdiction to hear appeals in criminal cases to the Court of Appeal: to amend the law relating to such appeals in England and Northern Ireland and appeals to the Courts-Martial Appeal Court: to amend the provisions of the Army Act 1955 and the Air Force Act 1955 relating to the powers of confirming officers: and for connected purposes."

c.40 Expiring Laws Continuance Act 1966.

"An Act to continue certain expiring laws."

c.43 Tribunals and Inquiries Act 1966.

"An Act to extend sections 1 and 7A of the Tribunals and Inquiries Act 1958 to further classes of statutory inquiries and hearings: to transfer to the Secretary of State the power to make rules of procedure under the said section 7A in respect of inquiries

and hearings in Scotland: to apply section 8 of that Act to procedural rules made by the Commissioners of Inland Revenue: to
make provision with respect to the attendance of members of the
Council on Tribunals at personal hearings under section 231 of the
Local Government Act 1933 and for purposes connected with the
matters aforesaid."

Naturally the length of an Act of Parliament will vary very
considerably depending upon the subject matter. The Companies
Act 1948 extends to some 459 sections: at the other extreme the
War Damage Act 1965 consists of 2 sections only.

(iii) *Public Bills.*—Although all Acts of Parliament have basically
the same form a distinction can be drawn between measures which
are introduced by the Government, those introduced by back-bench
Members of Parliament and those introduced by public bodies or
private citizens.

The most common type of legislation is the public bill. This is a
measure which affects the public at large and as would be expected
most such legislation is introduced to Parliament by the Government
through the Minister of the department which is particularly
concerned. To take some examples—the Minister of Transport
would introduce to and steer through Parliament legislation relating
to the construction of new motorways: the Minister of Housing and
Local Government, new subsidies for the building of council houses:
the Home Secretary, prison or police reforms; the Minister of
Health, changes in the National Health Service; the President of
the Board of Trade, grants and loans for regional development—
and so on. All these measures would affect the public by bringing
about some general change in the law and as such they would all be
classed as public bills. The procedure by which a public bill becomes
law will be dealt with in the following section of this chapter.

Every Act commences with the formal enacting clause which
shows the technical importance of the Royal Assent since the process
is made to seem the same as that which was used when the Monarch
really did govern.

"Be it enacted by the Queen's Most Excellent Majesty by
and with the advice of and consent of the Lords Spiritual and
Temporal and Commons in this present Parliament assembled
and by the authority of the same as follows:—"

The body of the Act then follows setting out in full the changes in
the law which are to take effect once the Act has been passed. The
rule is that the provisions become effective when the Act receives
the Royal Assent, unless some other arrangement has been made,

but it is now quite common for parts of an Act to come into force on different dates, sometimes on the making of an order by a central Government Minister.   The sections of the Act set out fully the changes to be effected in the law and if necessary sections are divided up into subsections.   Often the Act will end with an interpretation section which will define the important words and phrases: and then will follow any schedules.   A frequent example of a schedule is one which contains the list of repeal provisions, arising out of the new law;   another use of the schedule is for setting out the detailed constitution of a committee, board or tribunal set up under the Act in question.

The first illustration in Appendix A at the end of this book reproduces the opening page of the Tribunals and Inquiries Act 1958 and is a typical example of the appearance of legislation. Probably the most striking feature is that the law is set down in the fullest detail and in the most formal language possible.   The justification for this is the need for the utmost precision; after all the language used in the document will, once the necessary procedure has been followed, be the law.

(iv) *Private Bills.*—It has long been possible for public bodies and private individuals to apply for, and, in certain circumstances, obtain from Parliament a private Act of Parliament.   Such private Acts are sometimes classed as local Acts or personal Acts depending upon whether they affect a limited area or a particular family.   At the present time most such Acts are obtained by local authorities or similar public bodies but at one time in the past this method was one of the very few ways by which an individual could obtain a divorce.   The sort of purposes for which private Acts are obtained today appears from the following short list of such bills which were before Parliament early in 1967.   Most large local authorities obtain such powers in order to either make easier the task of local government in their area or to enable them to carry out some special project.

East Kilbride Burgh Bill
Brunel University Bill
Wallasey Corporation Bill
Edinburgh Corporation Order Confirmation Bill
Saint Barnabas, Lewisham Bill
Brighton Marina Bill
Tees Valley and Cleveland Water Bill
Port of London Bill

Bath University of Technology Bill
Mersey Docks and Harbour Board Bill

The name private bill is used because the bill is intended to have limited effect and is only to be of consequence to a particular group of persons or to a particular locality. In this limited objective it is, of course, quite the opposite of a public bill where the aim is to bring about a change in the general law. The procedure on an application for a private bill is also quite different from public bill procedure; nevertheless the form of a private Act is very similar indeed to the form of a public Act.

(v) *Difficulties facing Private Members' Bills.*—At the present time so much of Parliament's time is taken up with consideration of Government bills that very little opportunity is afforded for private Members to introduce bills with any hope of their measures becoming law. The bills which these back-bench Members of the House of Commons place before the House are public bills and they have to go through the same procedure as Government bills. Because of the time factor it has become an accepted practice for private Members to ballot for the right to introduce legislation but even those who are fortunate in the ballot have to rely on the goodwill of the Government to find the necessary time for the measure to go through the appropriate stages. In fact unless the Government is prepared to support the provisions in the bill it will almost certainly fail to become law. It is by no means uncommon for the Government to restrict severely the time available for private Members' bills in order to give its own legislation priority. The Murder (Abolition of Death Penalty) Act 1965 was introduced into Parliament by a private Member and passed through its various stages on a non-party basis. The Government assisted by finding the necessary time. Such instances are, however, not common since only some eleven bills introduced by private Members do, on average, become law each year and many of these are useful improvements but of very limited significance.

3 THE PROCEDURE FOR MAKING LEGISLATION

(a) Public Bill

(i) *Drafting.*—Inevitably the procedure begins with the drafting of the proposed bill. This is a highly skilled matter and is done by Barristers who are full time civil servants and who are expert at preparing draft legislation. They are known as Parliamentary Counsel. In the preparation they, naturally, consult closely with the civil servants of the central Government department whose Minister will be introducing the bill to Parliament, since the civil servants are the persons who will have to brief the Ministers who will be explaining and justifying the bill in Parliament.

(ii) *The Readings.*—Once prepared the bill is printed and on a suitable occasion the Clerk of the House of Commons reads the long title of the bill and it is given a formal first reading. (The term "reading" dates from the time when bills were actually read to the Members.) Copies are made available to Members and on an announced date a full-scale debate takes place on the general principles of the bill. At the conclusion of the debate the bill is either given a second reading or it is rejected. In practice Government bills are always carried, because the party machinery ensures that this is so. The bill then stands referred to its committee stage where it will be taken to pieces and examined clause by clause either by one of the standing committees of the House or, in the case of a bill of major importance, by the whole House sitting as a committee. In due course the bill as amended will be reported to the House, called the report stage, where further amendments are possible and then the final debate on the bill will follow known as the third reading at which stage only verbal amendments to the bill are permitted. The bill is then passed to the House of Lords where it undergoes a somewhat shorter but basically similar process.

This outline sketch of the legislative process takes no account of the practical realities of what is involved and in order to balance the account attention ought to be given to the role of the Opposition in the process. Almost certainly the political party which is in opposition will oppose the bill both in principle and in detail and will throughout do its best to point to the weakness in the Government's case and attempt wherever possible to gain political advantage. The press will see to it that debating points are fully reported and shortcomings by Ministers in defending the bill will be mercilessly exposed.

(iii) *Government tactics.*—If the Opposition attempt delaying tactics then the Government may adopt methods to place time limits on the particular stages of the bill. When this is done—called the closure, or the guillotine—much real or affected bitterness results and consideration of the bill tends to be somewhat haphazard. In such instances the review of the bill by the House of Lords which follows is a major advantage in that the amendments to the draft legislation can be looked at again without the same political rancour. It is in this connection that one can see the major difficulty which occurs with legislation and that is the need to produce it in detailed documentary form in the presence of a House of Commons some 630 strong in membership, the majority of whom are more interested in the political consequences of the bill than in the careful scrutiny which is essential if the legislation is not to be ambiguous. In the result judges are frequently engaged in interpreting Acts of Parliament.

(iv) *Omissions in Acts.*—The only consolation for the Government is that no matter what this interpretation may be, because of the supremacy of Parliament it is always possible for Parliament to pass another Act which will put the matter right. This tactic is seen clearly in relation to the decisions of the judges about matters of taxation each year. If a taxpayer discovers a loophole and the courts confirm that the taxpayer is right, in the next Finance Act, as one of its provisions, Parliament will take the opportunity to stop up that particular loophole. Similarly, if the courts give a decision on the law which Parliament is not prepared to accept, a change can be effected immediately by the making of a new Act of Parliament. The new Act may even be retrospective which again emphasises the supremacy of Parliament. However such legislation is much criticised. A recent instance of it occurred in 1965 when Parliament passed the War Damage Act to prevent the Government having to pay compensation to the Burmah Oil Company whose installations in Burma had been destroyed on Crown instructions during the 1939–1945 war. The House of Lords in its judicial capacity in *Burmah Oil Co.* v. *Lord Advocate* (1965) had held that the Crown under the Common Law had to pay compensation. Hence the War Damage Act was passed to change the law both for the future and retrospectively so that the Crown could escape the payment of this compensation.

(v) *Royal Assent.*—It will be noted that Parliament is made up of three constituent elements and no bill can become law without the giving of the formal Royal Assent by the third element in its composition, the Monarch. Time was when legislation issued direct from the Monarch. Today the Monarch plays a very minor role, since for some two hundred and fifty years the Royal Assent has been given without fail to bills which have successfully passed through the Commons and the Lords. The approval is signified by Lords Commissioners on behalf of the Monarch using the Norman French term "La Reine le veult"—the Queen wishes it. Thereafter the bill becomes an Act of Parliament and the law of the land.

(b) Private bill

(i) *Compared to public bills.*—A private bill is defined by the House of Commons Manual of Procedure as "a bill to alter the law relating to some particular locality or to confer rights on or relieve from liability some particular person or body of persons". Such a bill must go through the same process in both the Commons and the Lords as a public bill but there are two significant differences. First a private bill must be lodged with certain Parliamentary officers and special notice be given to any person likely to be affected by the bill's provisions, including the Minister of the central Government Department most closely concerned. There is thus a substantial procedural hurdle to be tackled before the bill is even permitted to start its course in Parliament. The second difference is that much use is made of small committees in Parliament's handling of such bills. Assuming that there is objection, and there almost always is or there would be no need for such bill at all, then a committee of four members of the Commons, or five members of the Lords, will hold what almost amounts to a judicial inquiry into the object and then the provisions of the bill. The object of the bill is vital since if the committee do not regard its object as desirable then the bill must fail. Even if its object is desirable there will be a detailed examination of its provisions. Ultimately the committee reports back to the House and if the report is favourable there is every likelihood that the bill will then get over the necessary procedural hurdles and become law.

The justifications for the method used are two. The committee saves the time of the House and party politics do not intrude into the matter: one grave disadvantage is the very high cost of putting through a private bill.

(ii) *Local authorities' private bills.*—Since local authorities are often promoters of private bills it would perhaps be revealing to consider the preliminary process which their measures must undergo in a little more detail. The power to promote or oppose a private bill is contained in the Local Government Act 1933 Part XIII. The first requirement is that the resolution to promote the bill must be carried by a majority of the whole number of councillors present at a council meeting of which ten clear days' public notice has been given. This public notice is given by newspaper advertisement and this enables an objector to submit his objection to the bill at once. The council's resolution is sent to the Minister for his approval and once this has been given the authority can deposit the bill in Parliament. However, before the Minister's approval is given, much discussion with Ministry officials takes place. Once the bill has been deposited in Parliament for fourteen days a further meeting of the Council must be held after another ten days' public notice has been given. The local authority must again by a majority of the whole number of the council confirm the propriety of the promotion. A failure to obtain such confirmation would result in the withdrawal of the bill.

(iii) *Support of the electorate.*—A further complication arises in the case of the submission of a private bill by a county borough, a non-county borough or an urban district council. Any of these authorities must after the deposit of the bill in Parliament hold what is called a town meeting to obtain the support of the local electorate. The details are to be found in schedule 9 of the Local Government Act 1933, which lays down that within seven days of the deposit, public notice by placards and local newspapers must be given, setting out the contents of the bill and convening a meeting within fourteen to twenty-eight days which all local electors may attend. At the meeting the bill in whole or in part must obtain the support of a majority of the electors present at the meeting. Whatever the resolution carried at the meeting a poll can be demanded by 100 electors or one-twentieth of the electorate or by the council. If the bill receives the local support of the meeting by resolution, it will proceed; if however a poll is demanded the bill's future rests with the outcome. There is even a statutory instrument to regulate the conduct of the poll which has to be held. All told a more cumbersome and unsatisfactory arrangement it would be difficult to devise: the county and rural district councils are fortunate to escape this preliminary difficulty.

Once the bill has obtained all the necessary resolutions of local support it must then, like any other private bill, undergo the process set out above.

(c) Private Member's bill

A private Member's bill will be a public bill and will as such undergo public bill procedure. The main differences are two: in the first place the private Member will be dependent on Government goodwill to find the necessary time for his measure in the well-filled Parliamentary time-table: and if the bill involves expenditure then the Member must have Government support since only a Minister can move the necessary financial resolution. Secondly the private Member has to make his own arrangements for drafting the bill. This, as will be gathered from the example given, is not an easy matter and calls for the services of specialist lawyers; presumably it can for this reason prove expensive.

(d) Provisional orders and special orders

In order to assist local authorities to obtain certain powers which are of a standard type there are two further methods available known as "provisional orders" and "special orders".

(i) *Provisional orders.*—A provisional order is an order made by a Minister of the Crown under the authority of an Act of Parliament. Such orders only take effect when included in a Provisional Orders Confirmation Act. The origin of such an order was the praiseworthy one of restricting the number of private bill applications made by local authorities. The intention was to have one set of provisions relating to, for example, a water undertaking, and then when a local authority needed such powers instead of applying to Parliament by private bill, the Minister concerned was able to submit a provisional order confirmation bill to Parliament containing the required powers for the particular locality. Since such a bill was nearly always a formality it did not take up much of the time of Parliament and it saved the local authority the expense of presenting a private bill. Today however such orders are not common.

The procedure under which local authorities obtain the powers in question is governed by section 285 of the Local Government Act 1933: the intention to make the order has to be advertised in the London Gazette and a local newspaper and if the Minister receives objections he will almost certainly hold a local inquiry. If the Minister decides to proceed he submits the order to Parliament for confirmation. Even then the objectors may by petitioning Parliament force the matter to be treated virtually on a private bill basis with a small committee holding a full inquiry. The order will then only become effective when Parliament has passed the bill.

(ii) *Special orders.*—Special orders are a form of delegated legislation since they are made by a Minister of the Crown who has been enabled to make such order by an Act of Parliament. The idea is for the Minister to confer powers on local authorities as necessary. The process is smooth if there is no opposition but where opposition occurs there is opportunity for the objection to be raised in the Commons and the Lords and again the hearing may result in the cumbersome private bill type of process. The Acts which govern this procedure are the Statutory Orders (Special Procedure) Acts 1945 and 1965.

(e) Consolidation and codification

(i) *Consolidating Acts.*—With the passage of time legislation can easily become complex and difficult. As the result of later amending legislation, with the consequent repeal of certain sections, the original, or principal, Act can become very confused. The only way to clarify the position is to have a new Act which will bring up to date all the various enactments affecting the legislation. Such an Act is called a consolidating Act.

Just such an Act is the Matrimonial Causes Act 1965 which has as its long title "An Act to consolidate certain enactments relating to matrimonial causes, maintenance and declarations of legitimacy and British nationality with corrections and improvements made under the Consolidation of Enactments (Procedure) Act 1949". The previous principal Act had been the Matrimonial Causes Act 1950 and between 1949 and 1965 no fewer than fifteen Acts and four Statutory Instruments had been passed which amended in some particular the 1949 Act. Thus with the passing of the 1965 Act the slate is, as it were, wiped clean. But this is, in turn, only temporary.

The number of consolidating Acts passed in the 1965 session numbered twelve out of some eighty-three Acts, and in bulk these twelve would make up more than half of the total number of pages on the statute book for the year. So consolidation can be seen to be an important activity of Parliament each year and the Consolidation of Enactments (Procedure) Act 1949 was passed so as to simplify the process by which such useful measures become law. The position under the Act is that the Lord Chancellor must prepare a memorandum explaining the need for the measure and setting out briefly the changes involved. A joint committee of both Houses considers the memorandum and provided that the committee recommends the measure as substantially reproducing the existing law it will then pass through the necessary stages in both Houses without debate.

(ii) *Codification.*—Consolidation is to be distinguished from codification which is not so common and which is the enactment of all the law on a particular subject including case law. This means that the resulting Act is likely to make substantial changes in the law. Examples are the Companies Act 1948, the Partnership Act 1890 and the Sale of Goods Act 1893. As an indication of what is involved in codification, the Bills of Exchange Act which became law in 1882 was built up from relevant material in 17 previous statutes and some

2,500 decided cases. Codification is thus much more complex than consolidation.

(iii) *Statute law revision.*—Codification again is to be distinguished from "statute law revision" which is the reprinting of statute law with the obsolete matter omitted: an example in 1965 was the Statute Law Revision (Consequential Repeals) Act 1965.

4 THE RELATIONSHIP BETWEEN THE HOUSE OF COMMONS, THE HOUSE OF LORDS AND THE MONARCH

(a) The Monarch

Because Britain remains a monarchy the Queen is the formal Head of State. However, the Monarch's position today is very much changed from that enjoyed by her various predecessors, since the course of history has seen a steady diminution in the powers of the Monarch with a corresponding increase in the powers of the elected representatives of the people. At the present time it is a well-understood convention of the constitution that the Monarch shall act only on the advice of her Ministers because in this way she can do no wrong. The only action in the legislative sphere with which she is connected is the giving of the Royal Assent to all bills which have passed through the House of Commons and the House of Lords. Here again the Assent is a formality since she is acting on the advice of her Ministers: just how formal this action is can be seen from the fact that the Royal Assent has not been refused in some two hundred and fifty years.

(i) *Relationship with Parliament.*—In the early days of Parliament the positions were reversed. The King governed and only called the Lords and Commons to attend to approve his proposed taxation. By way of a balance the Houses would ask for the "redress of grievances" and this left the King to decide whether or not to proclaim laws to meet the complaints. The choice was his. As time passed the Houses found it a more compelling method to prepare the legislation which they wanted and place it before the King for his approval. This explains why at the present day every Act of Parliament still begins "Be it enacted by the Queen's Most Excellent Majesty, by and with the advice of and consent of the Lords Spiritual and Temporal, and Commons, in this present Parliament assembled, and by the authority of the same as follows".

A second result of the history of Parliament is that the Monarch has the right to adjourn and dissolve Parliament; but once again in exercising this right she acts always on the advice of the Prime Minister of the day. In fact a Prime Minister is now expected to use the right to ask the Monarch to dissolve Parliament to his political party's advantage. That is he will ask for a dissolution when the party has the best chance of being returned to power with an increased majority. This choice must however be made within the five year period which is the maximum life of a Parliament.

(ii) *The Monarch and the Government.*—A third result is that at the opening of a new Parliament the Monarch begins the proceedings by reading the speech from the throne. This speech which is prepared by the Government but is read by the Monarch maintains the fiction that the Monarch is still the power in government. She will speak of "my" Ministers because as a fact the Government is known as Her Majesty's Government. It is because of this that the Monarch has the apparently important power of selecting "her" Prime Minister. The reality is of course that her choice is made for her by the political party which has won the election. Their acknowledged leader will become Prime Minister. There have been instances of the present Queen having to decide between two contestants for the leadership of the Conservative Party and hence the office of Prime Minister. Once when Sir Anthony Eden (as he then was) resigned when the choice was between Mr. Harold MacMillan and Mr. R. A. Butler, and again when Mr. Harold MacMillan resigned, between Lord Home (as he then was), Mr. R. A. Butler, Lord Hailsham (as he then was) and others. Some embarrassment was felt on both occasions although no blame attached to the Monarch, since she took appropriate advice before acting, but the position seems now to have been made clear that in future the leaders of the main political parties will be elected by the members of the party in the House of Commons and the Monarch will never again have to exercise personal choice.

Because the Prime Minister and his colleagues form "Her Majesty's Government" another constitutional requirement is that the Queen shall approve and formally appoint the Ministers to their respective offices. Today this formal task presents no difficulty.

(iii) *The Monarch's duties.*—Although the Queen plays only a formal part in the process of government she is bound to build up a sound knowledge of constitutional matters and she is kept informed both by receiving Cabinet Minutes and other State Documents and also by regular meetings with the Prime Minister. With increasing experience of office a Monarch's views are clearly of considerable value to the Government and this is sometimes expressed in the form that although the Monarch has no actual power, she has the right to be consulted, the right to encourage, and the right to warn.

The fictional discretionary powers which a Monarch is supposed to possess such as the right to adjourn and dissolve Parliament and the right to select the Prime Minister are often called Royal Prerogative powers. This expression "the Royal Prerogative" means those powers of government which are now in the personal discretion of the Monarch and are the residue of the absolute power which once belonged to the Monarch. Most such powers have been transferred to Parliament but some very significant powers remain *e.g.* the power to declare war and make peace, to enter into treaties, to create peers, and to give charters to Universities. But the important factor is that these prerogative powers are only exercised on the advice of the Government of the day. It would today be totally unconstitutional for a Monarch to attempt to exercise such a power without consultation.

(b) The House of Lords

The House of Lords has a longer history than that of the House of Commons since it was originally made up of those persons whose advice the Monarch became accustomed to take when he was considering matters of State. As the great land-owners of medieval times these were the feudal lords of the realm, the peers, as they became known. The custom early became established that the King would consult with his peers in the making of law, and the group soon built up its characteristic hereditary feature, as a result of which the eldest son of a peer automatically took his father's seat on his death.

(i) *Composition.*—The present House of Lords still consists substantially of hereditary peers of the realm known as the Lords Temporal but it has, additionally, the Lords Spiritual, who are 26 leading Anglican churchmen; there are also nine Lords of Appeal in Ordinary and an increasing number of life peers who like the bishops and the lawyers sit only for their own life-time. The life peers, created since the Life Peerages Act 1958, now number in the House about 130. There are both men and women and they are drawn from all walks of life. It is expected that the hereditary peers will be less in evidence as time passes since the hereditary principle is increasingly unacceptable in modern society as a criterion for government.

(ii) *The Parliament Acts.*—Until the Parliament Act 1911 the House of Lords played a vital part in the passage of new legislation.

Without its consent no bill could become law. It had an absolute veto. Because in 1909–1910 the House of Lords came into conflict with the House of Commons the Liberal Party then forming the Government fought an election on the basis that the power of the House of Lords to veto legislation should be substantially reduced. Following its success in the election the Liberal Government obtained the passage of the Parliament Act 1911 which reduced the complete veto of the House of Lords to a two years delaying veto over general measures and took it away altogether in relation to finance bills. In the Parliament Act 1949 the Labour Government then in power reduced the power of veto again from two years to one year and this remains the position. It should perhaps be added that the House of Lords has only exercised its veto since 1911 on very few occasions and at the present time it seems freely to acknowledge that it must give way to the wishes of the elected representatives of the people in the House of Commons. Where a bill becomes law without the approval of the House of Lords the formal enactment clause is amended to read "Be it enacted by the Queen's Most Excellent Majesty, by and with the consent of the Commons in this present Parliament assembled, in accordance with the provisions of the Parliament Acts 1911 and 1949, and by authority of the same as follows . . .".

(iii) *Functions.*—The functions of the House of Lords are to act as a revising chamber for all legislation coming from the House of Commons, to initiate non-controversial legislation, in appropriate circumstances to exercise their one-year veto so that public opinion can be expressed on the particular measure, and by debate to give a public airing to matters of current concern. The need for careful scrutiny of the draft legislation coming from the House of Commons has been mentioned before. The Government itself is often glad to introduce "second thought" amendments in the Lords also, so that this revision aspect is of real practical value. What is more, over the years the House of Lords has built up a reputation for constructive criticism and high standard debate in which the predominantly Conservative sympathies of the House have been tactfully subdued to its prior role as a legislative body. In matters of conflict the House of Lords has readily conceded that the decision of the House of Commons as the elected House must prevail and it seems unlikely that the House will ever again directly exercise its one-year veto save in a matter of extraordinary constitutional importance in what it saw as the vital interests of the nation. If this were to happen it is conceivable that the House of Commons might take away even the one-year veto. The initiation of comparatively non-controversial legislation as such codifying statutes as the Companies Act 1948 and the Justice of the Peace Act 1949, not only saves the time of the House of Commons but also allows the special skills of the Members of the House of Lords to be shown.

The one qualification in the Parliament Acts 1911–1949 which places the two Houses on an equal footing is in regard to any attempt by the House of Commons to extend its life-time beyond the five year limit there stipulated. No such bill can become law without the consent of both Houses and although in war-time such an extension has been agreed it can safely be said that it would only occur in an emergency.

(c) The House of Commons

Although historically the House of Commons might appear to be the junior element in Parliament the fact that it is the elected House has long since made it the senior body. For all practical purposes a decision of the House of Commons is tantamount to that decision becoming law. The logic being that what the majority party decides to be done is what the majority of electors in the country want done.

(i) *The Government and legislation.*—However the system under which the leading figures in the majority party in the House of Commons become after an election a cabinet under a Prime Minister results in the right to initiate legislation passing from the House of Commons to the Government. The back-bench Members of the majority party may agitate and criticise but once the Government insists on the need for the legislation the members will be forced to support it. This is not to deny that the back-bench Members can behind the scenes influence the Government but the point is that they have themselves very little chance of introducing legislation. The private Member's bill procedure which has been referred to above and which depends, irrespective of party allegiance, on first being successful in a ballot and second getting Government support means that the number of such bills actually becoming law in each Parliament is very few.

(ii) *Composition.*—The House of Commons consists of 630 elected members drawn from roughly equal size constituencies in England, Scotland, Wales and Northern Ireland. Members are elected on a political party basis and the party which wins the most seats at a general election forms the Government. Most of the legislation which will come from Parliament in the following years will be Government legislation, either giving effect to the expressed intentions of the party in the election campaign or regarded by the party as fulfilling the expectations of their supporters in the country.

(iii) *Place in the Constitution.*—The relationship which the House of Commons has with the Crown and with the House of Lords has been explained above. In matters of ceremonial it is still treated as the junior body since a representative group is sent for by Black Rod from the House of Lords to attend for such matters as the reading of the Queen's Speech from the throne, and the signifying of the Royal Assent to legislation. Even here the representatives from the House of Commons are treated as inferiors by being required to stand at the bar of the House of Lords for the proceedings. Judging from the recent mood of the House of Commons some change in this situation is regarded as overdue. (The Royal Assent Act 1967 does away with this procedure and allows the Royal Assent to be notified to the House through the Speaker.)

Nonetheless it is vital to an understanding of the making of legislation that it should be clearly understood that legislation can only be passed by the process explained above under which the three constituent elements of Parliament each play their part. No matter that the House of Commons has the real power, because not even it can make law on its own. In the case of *Bowles* v. *Bank of England* (1913), a budget resolution of the House of Commons imposing income tax at 1s. 2d. in the pound was held to be ineffective as law because it had not passed through the House of Lords and had not received the Royal Assent. As a result the Provisional Collection of Taxes Act 1913 was passed and this made proper provision for the House of Commons' budget resolutions to take effect immediately, subject to confirmation within a given time by the House of Lords followed by the Royal Assent.

The immense importance of the decisions of the House of Commons is thus somewhat hidden by the continued fiction of the supremacy of the Monarch and the superiority of the Lords Spiritual and Temporal. In the *Bowles* case just mentioned no-one suggested that the House of Lords or the Monarch might actually have refused their approval to the budget resolutions; it was simply that the ancient fiction of the Monarch's making of new legislation has to be played out to the full. The fiction, as has been seen, is particularly clear in the enactment clause which heads each Act of Parliament. It is carried even further in financial matters where the House of Commons deals with national income and expenditure. Because the Government is technically Her Majesty's Government the expenditure which it obtains approval for from Parliament is contained in Acts of Parliament which begin:

"Most Gracious Sovereign. We, Your Majesty's most dutiful and loyal subjects the Commons of the United Kingdom in Parliament assembled, towards making good the supply which we have cheerfully granted to Your Majesty in this Session of Parliament, have resolved to grant unto Your Majesty the sum hereinafter mentioned: and do therefore most humbly beseech Your Majesty that it may be enacted, and be it enacted by the Queen's Most Excellent Majesty, by and with the advice and consent of the Lords Spiritual and Temporal, and Commons, in this present Parliament assembled, and by the authority of the same, as follows:—"

This introduction must date from the very ancient past and has really no relevance today. The fiction, whilst otherwise harmless, does have one unfortunate by-product, however, and that is that a private member's bill which involves expenditure cannot pass the House of Commons unless a Government Minister on behalf of the Crown is willing to "demand" the expenditure from the Commons. The Commons must never be allowed to "offer" money to the Crown.

5 DELEGATED LEGISLATION

(a) General

Because Parliament has found itself so short of time in its tasks of discussing and enacting new law it has increasingly found it necessary to pass on its power to make law to certain other persons and bodies. The law which these other persons and bodies are thus able to make is known as delegated legislation, sometimes called subordinate legislation. This section of the chapter will be concerned with delegated legislation and in particular the forms which it can take.

The first point of importance is that when Parliament delegates its law making powers it does so subject to stringent conditions. Firm limits are set to the inferior body's power to make law so that there is no question of such a body having a free hand. Generally Parliament lays down the principles and the body in question deals with the detail.

(i) *Advantages.*—The advantages of the system are largely these:— it saves the time of Parliament in matters of detail and in the particular field in which it operates the person or body in question can bring great expertise to the making of the legislation. The disadvantages are the vast bulk of these detailed laws being produced under Parliament's authority and the fear that these persons and bodies, unlike Parliament, are not subject to effective democratic control. Whatever view is taken it is not possible to deny the need for delegated legislation because every year Parliament's legislative programme is very crowded.

(ii) *The various forms.*—Delegated legislation is likely to take one of three forms:—most important are the statutory instruments produced by central Government departments under the direct supervision of the appropriate Minister: then there are the orders in council made by the Monarch under Parliament's express authority: and finally the by-laws made by local authorities and public corporations. Each of these forms will now be considered in detail.

(iii) *Criticism.*—Delegated legislation is not a new thing but it is only in the twentieth century that it has become of considerable significance with the Government playing a so much greater part in the lives of everyone. At times the process has been heavily criticised. In the late 1920's Lord Chief Justice HEWART in a book called "*The New Despotism*" drew attention to the dangers as he saw them and such was the effect that in 1929 the Government set up a Committee on Ministers' Powers to look into delegated legislation and administrative tribunals. The 1932 report of this committee known as the Donoughmore Report confirmed the necessity of having delegated legislation and made for minor improvements. Misgivings have been voiced since this report nonetheless and the House of Commons has set up a standing committee known as the Select Committee on Statutory Instruments or "The Scrutiny Committee" to keep a check on such instruments.

(b) Statutory instruments

(i) *The 1946 Act.*—The term "statutory instrument" is comparatively new having been introduced by the Statutory Instruments Act 1946. Prior to that Act this form of delegated legislation had the title "statutory rules, orders and regulations". Under the 1946 Act the term "statutory instrument" is used to cover all forms of delegated legislation including orders in council where made under statutory authority and all are required on publication to be sent to the Queen's Printer, printed and numbered and made available for sale. An annual edition of statutory instruments is published and a complete set of volumes of all the statutory instruments in force is kept up to date by new issues. As new statutory instruments are being produced at the rate of 2,000 a year this is no simple task.

In Appendix A at the end of this book will be found an actual example of a statutory instrument. The illustration shows the opening page of the Town and Country Planning Appeals (Inquiries Procedure) Rules 1965, an important statutory instrument dealing with the procedure to be followed at a planning application inquiry.

(ii) *Statutory instruments, 1967.*—The following are examples of statutory instruments which were issued during the early months of 1967. They have been selected to show the range of matters which can be the subject of a statutory instrument.

1967   211 Cardiganshire Water Board Order 1967
        276 County Court (Amendment) Rules 1967
        212 Land Drainage (Grants) Regulations 1967
        261 Motor Vehicles (Tests) (Exemption) (Amendment) Regulations 1967
        321 Hampshire and Southampton (Boundaries) Order 1967
        330 National Insurance (Unemployment and Sickness Benefit) Regulations 1967
        394 Southern Rhodesia (Prohibited Trade and Dealings) (Amendment) Order 1967
        371 Bankruptcy (Amendment) Rules 1967
        432 Devon and Cornwall Police (Amalgamation) Order 1967
        442 Slaughterhouses (Meat Inspection Grant) (Revocation) Regulations 1967
        438 Parking Places and Controlled Parking Zone (Manchester) (1966) (Amendment) Order 1967

From these examples it is not difficult to grasp the immense range of topics which can be the subject of statutory instruments nor the way in which Parliament operates in this matter. As a principle, for example, it approves a new policy such as that redundancy payments shall be paid to workers who lose their jobs through redundancy. The detailed provisions are left to be drawn up and published by a Minister by way of a statutory instrument. Sometimes these details call for a number of statutory instruments covering the whole field of activity; this is particularly true in services having wide ramifications such as education or highways.

(c) **Orders in Council**

This term means orders made by the Monarch in her Privy Council, hence Orders in Council. With the Monarch's loss of personal powers over the years the making of orders in council has become a formality: such orders being made always on the advice of the Government of the day.

A distinction must be drawn between orders in council made under the authority of an Act of Parliament and those which are made under the ancient Crown prerogative. In both cases the formality by convention requires the Monarch's signature authenticated by those of the clerk and three Privy Councillors but Orders in Council made under Crown prerogative are not strictly a form of delegated legislation at all since they are exercised as of right without the need for Parliament's authorisation. Frequently this power would deal with legal matters affecting the Crown Colonies and Trust Territories and the regulation of trade and commerce in time of war. Again it must be stressed that this prerogative power is always exercised on the advice of the Government of the day.

In the case of orders in council made under Parliament's authority these are usually matters of constitutional significance. The order in council would seem to carry some extra authority. It is particularly useful in time of national emergency when Parliament gives very wide powers to the Government to deal with any situation which may arise. The speed with which such orders can be devised and promulgated is another major advantage as compared even with the normally flexible form of ministerial statutory instrument.

(d) **By-Laws**

Parliament also delegates its power to make law to various bodies. Of these bodies local authorities are the most important but it must not be overlooked that the various public corporations have power to make law for certain of their purposes too. Generally these laws are known as by-laws. The term comes from the old Norse word "by" meaning a town, so a by-law is, literally, a "town law".

It must not be assumed, however, that local authorities are entitled to make laws for their own areas more or less at their discretion. Parliament delegates the power it is true, but the power is delegated subject to the conditions specified in the Act and these are always very restrictive. For example a local authority is always required to submit its by-laws on any subject for confirmation by a central Government Department before they take effect, and this confirmation is not easily obtained.

(i) *Enabling powers.*—The power of local authorities to make by-laws is specifically given by individual statutes, *e.g.*:—

Act of Parliament	By-laws regulating the use of	Confirming authority
s. 19 Public Libraries and Museums Act 1964	libraries museums and art galleries	Secretary of State for Education and Science
s. 61 Food and Drugs Act 1955	markets maintained by a local authority	Minister of Housing and Local Government
s. 28 Small Holdings and Allotments Act 1908	letting allotments and generally	Minister of Agriculture Fisheries and Food
s. 46 Factories Act 1961	means of escape from fire in Factories	Minister of Housing and Local Government
Sch. 6 Weights and Measures Act 1963	sale of solid fuel	Minister of Power
s. 2 Ferries (Acquisition by Local Authorities) Act 1919	as to Ferries	Minister of Transport

A long list could be prepared of by-law making powers as bestowed by various statutes but additionally the general by-law making power bestowed by section 249 of the Local Government Act 1933 must be noted. This section enables county councils and borough councils to make by-laws for the good rule and government of their areas and for the suppression of nuisances. Clearly this is a very widely drawn section but limits are placed on the apparent powers of the local authorities by the requirement that such by-laws must be confirmed by a Secretary of State or other Minister before they take effect.

(ii) *Model codes.*—In practice what happens is that in all the by-law making fields the appropriate central Government Department prepares a model code of by-laws. Any local authority which submits by-laws which relate to or are adapted from the Model Code is likely to have its by-laws confirmed: if, however, it submits some original by-laws of its own devising, the chances are that confirmation will be refused.

The model code issued for by-laws for good rule and government and for the suppression of nuisances deals *inter alia* with such matters as:

noise nuisance from wireless loudspeakers: carrying carcasses: noisy animals: improper posting of advertising material: shooting galleries: fighting: the fouling of footpaths by dogs: flags: the use of foul language in a public place: advertising vehicles: nuisances contrary to public decency.

(iii) *Procedure for by-laws.*—The procedure which has to be followed by a local authority in making a by-law is generally covered by the procedure laid down in section 250 of the Local Government Act 1933.

This requires the draft of the proposed by-laws to be approved by the Council by the application of its common seal. The draft is then prepared for submission to whichever central government department is the confirming authority, often the Home Secretary or the Minister of Housing and Local Government, and at the same time public notice must be given by local newspaper advertisement of the intention to submit the by-laws for confirmation. Objectors have one month in which to express objection to the confirming authority. During this period copies of the proposed by-laws have to be made available for inspection at the council offices. The by-laws are then submitted and either confirmed with or without modification, or rejected by the confirming authority. Before arriving at its decision the confirming authority will check very carefully to see that the by-laws are "*intra vires*", that is within the by-law making powers given by the Act of Parliament to the local authority; also they will consider whether the proposed by-laws are necessary or not and finally that, so far as can be foreseen, the by-laws will not be found invalid by a court of law.

Once the by-laws are confirmed they will come into force on the date fixed by the confirming authority. The by-laws will be printed by the local authority and made available for sale at a cost not exceeding one shilling: where appropriate, for example, in the case of by-laws concerning the use of parks and open spaces, they will be printed in poster form and put on display.

It will be obvious that the need to use the model codes in the making of by-laws means that little initiative in the legislative sense rests with local authorities. It is even less than is apparent on the face of the actual legislation since at first sight it would seem that the power to make these local laws requires only formal consent from the named Minister for them to be effective. In practice it is comparatively rare for a local authority's suggestion for a new by-law to be accepted and, if it is accepted, it is solely because the Minister is prepared to allow it as an experiment.

6 LEGISLATION AND THE JUDICIARY

The role of the judiciary in relation to legislation can be simply stated as "interpretation". There is no power in the judiciary to refuse to implement an Act of Parliament since as has been seen earlier in this chapter Parliament is the supreme law-making body. This means that the only function of the judiciary in regard to legislation is to give a ruling as to the meaning of words or phrases whenever a case arises which calls for an interpretation.

The sort of difficulty which can come before a court can be illustrated from the case of a particular word or phrase: for example in affiliation proceedings it has been held that "a single woman" can include both a widow and a married woman living apart from her husband. Sometimes a particular phrase used in an Act gives rise to hundreds of cases. In the Workmen's Compensation legislation a person was entitled to a successful claim if the accident in which he was injured "arose out of and in the course of his employment". This phrase has had to be considered by judges in a great many cases.

(a) Statutory interpretation

Interpretation of this kind is then a major activity of the courts. The rules which a judge employs to assist him in this task are known as the rules of statutory interpretation. They can be summarised as:

(i) *The Golden Rule.*—The judge must interpret the word or phrase in question according to its ordinary, plain and natural meaning. This is sometimes also called the Literal Rule. The only qualification to this approach is that where a literal grammatical interpretation would result in absurdity or inconsistency within the statute or with the general law then the court will have to think again. The over-riding problem in all these cases is the difficulty that arises with language. Even the simplest words can in certain circumstances prove extremely difficult to interpret: what, for example, is "furniture"? and how much "furniture" is necessary to warrant the description a "furnished letting"? In two different cases the meaning in the context of the words "of" and "at" in Acts of Parliament have been the crux of the difference between the parties.

(ii) *The Mischief Rule.*—If the Golden Rule does not help the judge he may apply what has come to be known as the Mischief Rule. This rule is so called because the judge will look at the previously existing mischief which the statute in question is intended to remedy and interpret the word or phrase in question accordingly.

It will be noticed that the judge is restricted to the actual words of the Act of Parliament. He is not permitted to enquire behind the Act as to what was said in Parliament by way of explanation when the Bill was being discussed nor to refer back to any committee report on which the legislation is based. It is felt that the use of these "extrinsic aids" would introduce too much latitude and lead to a lowering of drafting standards by Parliament. The judges have often stated their view that if Parliament does not agree with their interpretation of the Statute then it is always open to it to pass a new Act to put the matter right.

(iii) *The "Eiusdem Generis" Rule.*—Where general words follow particular words the general words are interpreted in the light of the particular words which precede. In *Simpson* v. *Teignmouth Bridge Company* (1903) a local Act authorised a bridge toll on the following vehicles: "coach, chariot, hearse, chaise, berlin, landau and phaeton, gig, whiskey, car, chair, or coburg, and every other carriage hung on springs". It was held that a bicycle was not within the Act. Similarly in *Evans* v. *Cross* (1938) the Road Traffic Act then in force defined a "traffic sign" as including "all signals, warning sign posts, direction posts, signs or devices". It was held that a white painted line on a road was not a traffic sign since "devices" had to be construed "*eiusdem generis*" with the foregoing words.

(iv) *Other rules and presumptions applied by judges.*—Where the statute contains a list of specific matters not followed by any general words then the judge will limit the Act to the specific matters listed. This is known as "*expressio unius est exclusio alterius*" (the expression of one thing implies the exclusion of another).

The meaning of a word or phrase can sometimes be obtained by a study of its place in the general context of the Act. This is known as "*noscitur a socciis*".

The following presumptions are made:

(1) against an alteration of the existing law unless **expressly** stated
(2) that the statute does not bind the Crown
(3) that the statute does not have retrospective effect
(4) against restriction of private liberty, and
(5) against the imposing of taxation unless the statute is clear.

(b) Control over delegated legislation: judicial and parliamentary

The major method of control by the judiciary over delegated legislation is the straightforward one that such legislation must be made completely within the authorisation given under the Act of Parliament which enables it to be made. The courts will intervene to declare ineffective any delegated legislation which is beyond the powers (*"ultra vires"*) of the person or body making it. There are two grounds on which the courts may hold that the Parliamentary authority has been exceeded, procedural *ultra vires* and substantive *ultra vires*.

(i) *Procedural ultra vires.*—This means that if the procedure required to be followed by the enabling statute has not been followed exactly then the delegated legislation made will be held to be invalid. Examples of where such a failure might occur are (1) where a statutory instrument is required to be laid before Parliament and has not been so laid (2) where the required consultation before making the instrument has not taken place, provided that the consultation was compulsory and not discretionary (3) where the instrument has not been signed by or on behalf of the Minister who is required to sign it.

(ii) *Substantive ultra vires.*—This means that if the delegated legislation is not expressly or impliedly authorised by the Act in question (often called "the parent Act") or if it conflicts with other legislation, then on either of these grounds it can be held to be void as *"ultra vires"*. Thus in one case, *Hodge* v. *Hodge* (1963), a statutory instrument was held to be *"ultra vires"* because it required a party to take a procedural step in an action which conflicted with the provisions of the parent Act. Again in *Attorney-General* v. *Wilts United Dairies* (1922), a fee imposed on the issue of a licence was held to be *"ultra vires"*; there was power to issue a licence but no power to charge a fee.

In practice few cases actually occur, but this may be as a result of the caution of the persons and bodies having power to make delegated legislation, in the knowledge that any excess of power is likely to bring in its train immediate intervention by the courts. Added to this caution is the very obvious care which Parliament itself exercises in bestowing the power to make delegated legislation.

(iii) *Parliamentary control.*—This involves, apart from the conditions laid down in the parent Act, first, the supervision of printing and publication as a result of the Statutory Instruments Act 1946:

secondly, the actual scrutiny of having certain instruments laid before Parliament. This means that in some instances the Houses have to give their blessing by affirmative order before the instrument takes effect, and in other instances the instrument will take effect unless it is annulled by an order of either House within a given period of time, usually forty days. Finally there is the work of the Select Committee on Statutory Instruments which is charged with the responsibility of drawing the House of Commons' attention to any instrument which falls within any of these categories:

(1) that it imposes a tax or charge
(2) that it could not be challenged in the courts
(3) that it makes some unusual or unexpected use of the delegated power
(4) that there has been unjustified delay in the publication or laying of the instrument
(5) that it would apply retrospectively
(6) that it has not been properly laid, and
(7) that it is obscure and requires elucidation.

Another rather different aspect of the relationship between the courts and delegated legislation arises from the duty of interpretation which exists and which is carried out in exactly the same way as the courts' task in interpreting an Act of Parliament.

(c) Judicial examination of by-laws

Earlier in this chapter examples were given of the by-law making powers of local authorities together with an outline of the procedure which is required to be followed before a by-law becomes law.

In this section a survey will be made of the role of the courts in relation to cases arising out of by-laws. The first point to note is that just because the confirming authority approves the by-laws submitted by the local authority that does not mean that the by-laws cannot be questioned in a court of law. In fact there are a number of grounds on which the courts may hold by-laws to be invalid.

(i) *Intra vires.*—First of all the court will look at the by-law under consideration to ensure that it is "*intra vires*", within the powers delegated, and that the proper statutory procedure has been followed exactly in the making of the by-law. A failure on either ground would make the by-law invalid, but in regard to the procedural aspect section 252 of the Local Government Act 1933 lays down that there shall be a presumption that a printed copy of the by-laws, signed by the clerk of the local authority, has been properly made and confirmed.

A case which shows exactly the distinction in this context between a by-law made "*intra vires*" and one made "*ultra vires*" is *R*. v. *Wood* (1855). There the power to make by-laws for health purposes extended to cover a requirement that an occupier should remove "dust, ashes, rubbish, filth, manure, dung and soil". A by-law which required an occupier to remove snow from the footpath outside his premises was held to be "*ultra vires*" and therefore ineffective.

(ii) *Reasonableness*.—A further test of the validity of a by-law is that of reasonableness. This is a deliberately vague test which leaves a discretion in the court to allow or disallow a by-law where it considers that the by-law goes beyond what Parliament intended.

In *Arlidge* v. *Islington Corporation* (1909) a by-law power "for the cleansing and lime washing at stated times" of houses let in lodgings was held to be unreasonable where the by-law made required land-lords to "cause every part of such premises to be cleansed in the month of April, May or June in every year". Lord Chief Justice ALVERSTONE said: "An absolute duty is imposed on every landlord to cause the premises to be cleansed and a penalty is imposed for breach of that duty when the landlord may be quite unable to carry out the work without breaking a contract or committing a trespass. The by-law is therefore unreasonable and bad".

In *Parker* v. *Bournemouth Corporation* (1902) a by-law power for regulating the selling or hawking of articles for sale on a beach or foreshore was held to be unreasonably exercised by a by-law which forbade such selling or hawking "except in pursuance of an agreement with the corporation". The effect of this exception was unreasonable because it attempted to make the corporation sole arbiter of any agreement made and because also it went beyond the power of regulation to the state of prohibition. Hence the by-law was unreasonable and invalid.

In *Kruse* v. *Johnson* (1898) a by-law was considered which prohibited "any person from playing music or singing in any place within fifty yards of any dwellinghouse after being requested to desist". The Queen's Bench Divisional Court found that the by-law was reasonable and gave a careful statement of the test of "reasonableness" from which the following rules emerge:

(1) by-laws made by local authorities should be supported if possible

(2) it is the local authority who should exercise the discretion and not the judge: "a by-law is not unreasonable merely because particular judges may think that it goes further than is prudent or necessary or convenient, or because it is not accompanied by a qualification or an exception which some judges may think ought to be there"

(3) the word "unreasonable" must be considered along similar lines to the rules of natural justice: is the by-law partial and unequal as between classes? is it manifestly unjust? does it disclose bad faith? is it an unjustifiably oppressive or gratuitous interference with the rights of those affected by it?

A court is only entitled to find a by-law unreasonable if its conclusion is that Parliament never intended to give authority to make such a rule and that it is therefore *"ultra vires"* (*per* Lord Chief Justice RUSSELL).

(iii) *Certainty.*—A further test of a by-law which is imposed by the courts is whether or not the by-law is certain in its terms: that is it must be quite clear as to the persons who are to be subject to it and quite clear also as to what it is that that person is required to do or not to do. In *Nash* v. *Finlay* (1901) a by-law which stipulated that "no person shall wilfully annoy passengers in the streets" was held to be uncertain and void. Again in *Scott* v. *Pilliner* (1904) a by-law which imposed a penalty on any person frequenting and using any street or public place "for the purpose of selling or distributing any paper or written or printed matter devoted wholly or mainly to giving information as to the probable result of races, steeplechases or other competitions" was held to be uncertain and void. The court felt that there might well be innocent sales of such papers and that the by-law was too widely drawn.

(iv) *Consistency.*—Finally a by-law must not clash with existing principles of law. If it does it is invalid as being inconsistent with or repugnant to common law, or as dealing with a matter already covered by statute law. In *Powell* v. *May* (1946) a by-law which prohibited betting in a public place was invalid because it attempted to prohibit the doing of an act which the existing statute law expressly or impliedly allowed. In *London Passenger Transport Board* v. *Sumner* (1935) there was an attempt to prosecute a passenger under a by-law for travelling on a bus without paying her fare. The by-law attempted to place on the passenger the responsibility for paying "the fare legally demandable". The passenger in question had paid a fare but had travelled beyond that fare stage; when challenged she was willing to pay the additional fare. The court held that the by-law was invalid as being in conflict with the common law principle that "mens rea" (a guilty mind) must be present for a crime to be committed.

This rule about consistency only applies to a conflict and not to by-laws which are supplementary provisions and which may extend the existing law. Most by-laws are, in fact, to be seen as supplementing the existing law.

Chapter 3

The Making of Law in the Courts

1 INTRODUCTION

The last chapter looked at how the law is made by Parliament. It is a simple matter to see how this is done because any one can go to a bookshop and buy a copy of an Act of Parliament. Such Acts of Parliament are all making new law and although over the years the number of Acts passed in each session of Parliament has not increased markedly, what has increased is the length and the complexity of the Acts. From an average annual total of 335 pages on the statute book in the 1906–13 sessions of Parliament the number had risen to 1,451 pages in 1959. In addition the new law made under the authority of Parliament as delegated legislation must also be reckoned with as part of the annual output. In recent years over 2,000 statutory instruments have been published each year and in terms of pages this means that substantially more new law is made annually as delegated legislation than as legislation. The combination of such law made by Parliament, whether directly or indirectly, is clearly a major source of new law today.

At the same time a very important contribution to the making of law continues to be made by the courts. All through history the judges have been called upon to decide between conflicting views by way of a reasoned judgment explaining the principles of law on which that decision is based. This role is even older in origin than the making of law by Parliament since this country had a firmly established system of law long before it had a Parliament. This chapter will be concerned with the way in which the judges in their courts make law. First a study of the court structure will be necessary; this is so because to understand the treatment of the different types of case it is essential to be able to distinguish between the civil and the criminal court structure and to recognise the place in the structure of the individual courts. This is particularly the case because of the emphasis placed on the doctrine of judicial precedent whereby the status of the court largely governs the authority of the judgment given. (See chapter 1. Sources: case law.) Besides a knowledge of the structure it is also desirable that an understanding should then be obtained of the procedure followed in the courts. For instance there is a contrast between the major part played by the jury in a criminal trial, where the judge acts only as a sort of chairman, elucidating and explaining the law and summarising the facts to assist the jury to reach its verdict, and its increasing absence in civil cases where, more often than not, trial is before a judge alone and the argument is more likely to be related to the legal principles to be applied. Again there is a marked contrast between the trial of a case at first instance where the parties and the witnesses play a prominent part and give their evidence, and the procedure on appeal where the appeal court judges will deal only with the technical points of appeal and witnesses are unlikely to be called. Since the activity in each court is quite different and is intended to suit the court's particular purpose, an understanding of the structure alone would not be adequate. The final section of the chapter will be a study of the role of the judge and in particular of the way in which he reaches his decision and how that decision may affect existing legal principles in that field of law. In this matter the various fields of civil law are much more in point than the criminal law, where basic issues are almost always of fact and are decided by a jury. It is possible to have arguments on points of law in a criminal case but such cases are the exception; whereas in civil law thousands of cases annually set posers for judges as to the legal principles to be applied, and of these cases those which are thought to be the most important decisions are placed on record in full by publication in the law reports (see Appendix B for an extract from a judgment to illustrate how the judge gives a reasoned explanation for his decision).

2　THE ORGANISATION AND JURISDICTION OF THE CIVIL COURTS

(a) The county court

For over one hundred years, since the County Courts Act 1846, the lowest court in status in the hierarchy of the civil court structure has been the county court. This court deals, on a local basis, quickly and cheaply with civil actions in matters of limited significance. Since claims for £500 or less are heard in this court its main function is to deal with vast numbers of debt cases: another important aspect of its work is in disputes between landlords and tenants mainly about a landlord's right to take possession of the house or the flat which he has previously let to a tenant.

Diagram of the organisation of the Civil Court Structure:

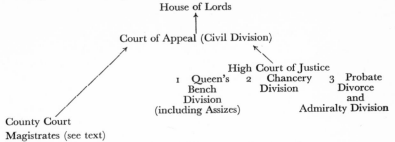

House of Lords

Court of Appeal (Civil Division)

High Court of Justice

| 1 Queen's Bench Division (including Assizes) | 2 Chancery Division | 3 Probate Divorce and Admiralty Division |

County Court

Magistrates (see text)

N.B. The arrows represent the possible course of an appeal.

(i) *The circuits.*—So that the court will be truly a local court and will be able to give an immediate hearing and decision the county court system has been built on a circuit basis. The country has been divided into approximately sixty-three circuits in each of which there will be a number of towns in which a county court will be held on one or more days a month. Altogether there are over four hundred such towns. In the largest cities the circuit will consist of the one court only, sitting continuously, and possibly having two judges serving it; whereas in a sparsely populated rural area there may be a dozen towns to be visited in the course of the month. The system is flexible and as population changes take place the increased weight of business will be met by a change in the circuit arrangements or, if necessary, even by a change in the circuit itself. The name county court is in itself misleading in that the system is not based on the geographical or the administrative county; often one circuit will cover towns in several different counties.

(ii) *The judges.*—Each circuit has at least one judge appointed to it. At present there are seventy-nine such judges and there is provision for up to ninety. The appointment is made by the Crown through the Lord Chancellor or for the appropriate area by the Chancellor of the Duchy of Lancaster, and the person appointed continues in office at a salary of (at present) £5,775 per annum until the age of 72, or exceptionally, 75. He, or she, will be a former practising barrister with at least seven years' experience as an advocate. Unlike the senior judges who are virtually irremovable, the county court judge can be removed from office by the Lord Chancellor for serious misconduct or incompetence. In court the judge, who wears wig and robe, is easily identified by the purple sash which he wears over his robe. He is addressed as "Your

Honour" and deals with cases without a jury. A jury of eight may be called but is, in practice, very rare. Solicitors and barristers may appear as advocates in this court, but above this level only barristers have the right of audience. Solicitors do not wear wigs, barristers do, so in court the distinction is clear.

The administration of each court circuit is carried out by a Registrar, who is a solicitor of at least seven years' standing, assisted by clerical staff. The registrar can himself hear cases where the amount involved is less than £30. An appeal from his decision lies to the judge.

In 1965 approximately one and a half million cases were started in the county court: of these only 4 per cent reached the trial stage because most claims were met or settled or abandoned by agreement between the parties, but the very large number of cases started there explains the reason why the county court is sometimes called "the most important court in the land".

(iii) *Jurisdiction.*—The law affecting county courts is to be found in the County Courts Act 1959 which sets out the full details of jurisdiction and procedure. The more important work of the court (called its jurisdiction) can be summarised as:

> actions founded on contract and in tort not exceeding £500 (but not libel, slander, seduction or breach of promise which are almost always tried in the High Court)
>
> actions concerning land of a rateable value up to £400
>
> equity matters concerning for example, trusts, mortgages or partnerships where under £500 is involved
>
> admiralty cases (some courts), i.e. shipping cases £1,000 maximum, raised in salvage cases to £3,500 maximum
>
> Probate disputes where the deceased person's estate is valued at less than £1,000
>
> bankruptcy (some eighty courts) unlimited jurisdiction—but not in London where the Chancery Division of the High Court has jurisdiction
>
> company winding up where the capital of the company is less than £10,000
>
> miscellaneous functions connected with—adoption, guardianship of infants and legitimacy.

A complication is added by the fact that if the parties wish it, the financial limits can be waived and the case heard in the county court: again if the claim, although under £500 involves an unusual point of law or fact, the judge can permit it to be transferred to the

High Court. If a plaintiff insists on taking his case to the High Court he runs a risk that the High Court may only allow him, even if he wins, to recover costs on the lower county court scale, and as such he may be out of pocket. The High Court actively discourages the bringing of cases to it which could be tried in the county court. It even remits cases to the county court where the amount claimed is more than £500 if it considers that the matter could as well be heard there.

(iv) *Divorce cases.*—Under the Matrimonial Causes Bill introduced in 1967, certain county courts are to be designated as divorce courts and all petitions for divorce will be brought to the county court in the first instance. If the petition is undefended the county court can hear the case, but if defended the case will have to be transferred to the High Court. The county court will be able to deal with claims for maintenance and the custody of the children arising in cases where it has heard the petition for divorce.

(v) *Appeals.*—Appeal from the judge's decision in the county court is to the Court of Appeal (Civil Division). There are, naturally some limits to the right of appeal. On a point of law one can appeal if the claim is for more than £20; and on fact one can appeal if the claim is for more than £200. Even on lesser claims with leave of the judge or the Court of Appeal an appeal may be brought.

(b) The magistrates

At this point it is necessary to clarify the position of the magistrates' courts in the civil court structure. It is a fact that the magistrates have jurisdiction in some civil cases. This derives for reasons of history from the time when magistrates played an important part in local administration. They thus hear appeals in certain disputes between local authorities and the individual. For example, assessment notices for the making up of a private street under the Private Street Works Code, applications relating to the diversion or "stopping up" of highways and rights of way, to enforce the payment of rates due, and nuisance abatement notices. They also deal with the law relating to licensed premises, with domestic proceedings between a husband and a wife, usually over maintenance, with affiliation order proceedings, and with children and young persons in need of care and protection. All these matters are dealt with either at the court of summary jurisdiction or at quarter sessions but important though the topics are, they do not, it is generally agreed, amount to enough to warrant classifying the magistrates as a civil court.

(c) The High Court of Justice

Above the limits laid down for the county courts, cases are heard in the High Court. The High Court has three branches or divisions each having its own well-defined jurisdiction. This court was established in the general reconstruction brought about by the Judicature Acts 1873 and 1875 when the High Court and the Court of Appeal were together created as the Supreme Court of Judicature. The present three divisions date from 1880.

(i) *The judges.*—Judges in the High Court can number sixty-three. They are appointed by the Queen on the recommendation of the Lord Chancellor and they are selected from the ranks of experienced practising barristers. The minimum requirement is ten years' experience. They are technically called "puisne" judges, the word "puisne" meaning "junior" or "inferior" presumably by comparison with the Appeal Court judges. In court they wear wig and robe and are addressed as "Your Lordship". Generally the judge sits alone but he may for certain purposes have the assistance of a jury. Because a county court judge and a High Court judge has no appeal function such courts are often called "courts of first instance".

On appointment the Lord Chancellor allocates the judge to one particular division of the High Court but he can be asked to serve in any division. By convention a knighthood is always bestowed on the new judge and the salary is £10,000 per annum. Once appointed a judge can only be removed from office by an address to the monarch from both Houses of Parliament requesting his removal. In addition the salaries of High Court and Appeal Court judges are secured on the national revenues and are not voted annually by Parliament. These provisions are a relic of the constitutional struggle of the seventeenth century as a result of which the monarch lost the personal right to appoint and dismiss judges. Today every effort continues to be made to secure the independence of the judges from the influence of the Crown and the government of the day.

The three divisions of the High Court to the work of each of which attention must now be given are the Queen's Bench Division, the Chancery Division and the Probate Divorce and Admiralty Division.

(ii) *The Queen's Bench Division.*—This division, the descendant of the common law courts, is the largest in number of judges and is presided over by the Lord Chief Justice. The present number of judges is thirty-six.

The jurisdiction is complex because Queen's Bench Division judges try at first instance both civil cases and criminal cases, and they are also called upon to furnish a divisional court and to assist in the work of the Court of Appeal (Criminal Division).

Although in its civil jurisdiction the High Court has unlimited jurisdiction the work of the division can be briefly stated as, in general, all claims arising in contract or tort above the county court limit of £500. This accounts for a vast number of cases since motor vehicle and factory accidents where serious personal injuries are suffered and all substantial breaches of contract will frequently lead to claims of over £500.

These civil cases are heard either at the law courts in the Strand in London or at the assize towns which form such an important element in the criminal court structure (see next section: assizes). Since the criminal business has priority, the number of civil cases heard at assizes is limited, but wherever the matter is heard, one judge sits to try the case and he may be assisted by a jury of twelve if this is requested and he agrees. Jury trial is, however, becoming increasingly uncommon in civil cases. At actions for trial in London and Middlesex in 1965, only 38 cases out of 807 were tried by jury in the Queen's Bench Division and most of these would be concerned with alleged wrongs to personal reputation such as libel and slander.

The Queen's Bench Division also provides the judge for what is known as the Commercial Court where banking, insurance and other cases are tried under a speedy informal procedure designed to obtain an urgent authoritative decision. It further provides some of the judges for the Restrictive Practices Court where, with the assistance of certain specially appointed laymen, investigations are held under the Restrictive Trade Practices Act 1956 and the Resale Prices Act 1964 into restrictive trade agreements, e.g. price fixing agreements. The court's object is to discover whether or not the agreements can be justified in the public interest and if not to declare them void. (In 1965, the court had before it some 176 notices of reference for hearing).

The administrative work of the division is controlled by eight barristers known as Masters of the Queen's Bench Division and they also supervise the Central Office of the Supreme Court.

(iii) *The Chancery Division.*—This division is the successor of the old system of equity and for this historical reason is presided over in name by the Lord Chancellor although he never sits. Cases are heard only in London at the law courts and at present nine judges are assigned to this division.

The jurisdiction is varied but the following are among the Chancery Division's more important functions:

the execution of trusts
the redemption and foreclosure of mortgages
the dissolution and accounts of partnership
the administration of the estates of deceased persons
the wardship of infants
revenue disputes, *i.e.* tax matters
company law matters

It is noteworthy that many Chancery cases are not so much disputes as matters requiring a legal determination or interpretation: for example, the carrying out of the provisions of a trust or the reconstruction of a company's capital arrangements. For this reason a jury is not used. The barristers who appear in Chancery cases are specialists in Chancery practice and the judges who are assigned to this division are drawn from their ranks. The administrative work which tends to be very detailed, particularly in the drawing up of court orders and the taking of accounts, is handled by seven solicitors known as Chancery Masters.

Since Chancery takes its name from the Lord Chancellor's court (see chapter 1: History of Equity) this would seem to be the appropriate place to consider the office of Lord Chancellor. He is the head of the judiciary but unlike all the other judges his appointment is a political one since he is a cabinet minister and goes out of office with the government of which he is a member. In addition to being in charge of a department, the Lord Chancellor is also a prominent figure in the House of Lords, where he sits on the Woolsack and acts both as a sort of chairman and as a government spokesman. There can hardly be a more exacting office.

(iv) *The Probate, Divorce and Admiralty Division.*—The three fields of law which are quite arbitrarily joined to form this division are linked only as a result of history. Probate, which is the obtaining of a legal title to administer a deceased person's estate, and divorce, the termination of the status of marriage between two persons, both belonged until the middle of the nineteenth century to the Church. The admiralty jurisdiction which developed on an international basis incorporated much Roman law and was long regarded as a separate jurisdiction. In the reconstruction of the courts in 1873–1875, because of the common link with Roman law and also because these three fields of law did not fit in elsewhere, they were associated together to form one of the divisions of the High Court.

Hence the rather surprising union of what A. P. Herbert has called "the three wrecks"—wrecks of wills, of marriages, and of ships.

The division is presided over by the President of the Probate, Divorce and Admiralty Division and he is assisted by sixteen judges.

The Probate jurisdiction involves the granting of documentary authority to a named person or persons to deal with the estate of a deceased person. This authorisation takes the form either of a probate where there is a will, or letters of administration where no will has been made. Once this authority has been given, the person named, who is called the personal representative, is able to wind up the estate of the deceased and distribute the balance available in accordance with the terms of the will or, when there is no will, under the statutory rules of intestacy. Some 200,000 grants of probate and letters of administration are made each year. These are dealt with by the Probate Registries which are to be found in various large cities and it is only in cases of considerable difficulty, or where the proving of the will is contested, that a hearing before a judge will be necessary.

The Divorce jurisdiction has increased enormously since 1945 and special arrangements have had to be made to deal with the numbers involved. In 1966 nearly 43,000 petitions for the dissolution of marriage (divorce) were filed. Special divorce commissioners (often the local county court judge) are appointed to hear undefended cases at the local assize towns and in London. This leaves the High Court judges free to take defended cases or cases of unusual complexity. They too go on the assize circuits for this purpose. The conditions which Parliament requires to be complied with before a divorce can be granted have brought about some very involved legal distinctions in this field of law. In addition to divorce petitions the jurisdiction extends to decrees of nullity, judicial separation and for the restitution of conjugal rights. The Matrimonial Causes Bill introduced in 1967 proposes to transfer the divorce jurisdiction to the county court although all defended cases must, and any other case can, be transferred to this division of the High Court for determination.

The Admiralty jurisdiction takes in all aspects of maritime law; in particular collisions at sea, salvage claims and, in time of war, prize cases. The law is derived from Roman law adapted by the practices which became established with international trade. It is a highly specialised branch of law and the judge can call for the assistance of nautical assessors from Trinity House on technical issues. A jury is not used. One unusual feature is that proceedings can be taken against a ship instead of against a person, called *"in rem"* as against *"in personam"*; and thus a writ can be nailed to the mast and departure of the ship prevented. As a result cases are known by the name of the ship the subject of the action.

(d) Divisional courts

Each division of the High Court also has a divisional court which, generally speaking, is concerned with appeals.

(i) *Queen's Bench Divisional Court.*—The Queen's Bench Divisional Court is the best known having two particularly important functions. First it hears many criminal cases where the appeal is on a point of law (see next section: Queen's Bench Divisional Court) and second it has a supervisory role over the activities of all courts and tribunals which are inferior in status to it. It is in this second capacity that it is of considerable consequence in a study of public law. Any complaint by an aggrieved party, at the conduct of a court or tribunal and seeking the quashing of the lower court or tribunal's decision, is heard by a Queen's Bench Divisional Court. It is also the court which deals with applications for the writ of *habeas corpus* where a person has been improperly detained. In chapter 5 where the control of the courts over the decisions of administrative bodies is considered, this divisional court will frequently be referred to.

The court is composed usually of three judges with the Lord Chief Justice presiding. For certain purposes two judges will suffice but for trials three normally form the court.

(ii) *Chancery Divisional Court.*—A divisional court of the Chancery Division is made up of two Chancery Division judges and hears appeals from decisions of a county court judge in bankruptcy matters. It may also hear appeals from the Industrial Insurance Commissioner and in matters concerning settled land and land registration.

(iii) *Probate, Divorce and Admiralty Divisional Court.*—A Divisional Court of the Probate, Divorce and Admiralty Division is made up of two Probate, Divorce and Admiralty Division judges. This court is kept busy hearing many appeals from decisions of the magistrates exercising their jurisdiction in domestic proceedings. A less frequent type of appeal is where a decision cancelling or suspending the certificate of a master, mate or engineer, arising from an investigation into his conduct or into a shipping casualty, has been made under the Merchant Shipping Act 1894.

(e) The Court of Appeal (Civil Division)

The Court of Appeal on its civil side hears appeals from the County Courts and from the three divisions of the High Court of Justice including divisional courts and civil assize cases. It was established together with the High Court of Justice as the Supreme Court of Judicature by the Judicature Acts 1873-1875. The actual head of the civil side is the Master of the Rolls and he is assisted by eleven Lords Justices of Appeal. The usual practice is for three judges to sit to hear an appeal and the court may in consequence sit in up to four divisions simultaneously. In 1965 the court dealt with 659 cases of which 164 came from the county courts. The appeal is not a re-hearing of the case, no witnesses are called and there is no jury: argument takes place only on the particular point or points of appeal. Judgment usually follows some time after the hearing, each judge explaining his own decision. The judges are all barristers who are required to have had at least fifteen years' experience or have been puisne judges and they are paid £10,000 per annum. The Master of the Rolls, the Lords Justices of Appeal (and the Lords of Appeal in Ordinary in the House of Lords) together with the Lord Chief Justice and the President of the Probate, Divorce and Admiralty Division, who are ex-officio members of the Court, are all appointed by the Queen on the advice of the Prime Minister. Most appointments are made from the High Court bench.

(f) The House of Lords

(i) *Jurisdiction.*—The House of Lords in its judicial capacity is the supreme appeal court in cases both civil and criminal in England and Wales but it only takes cases involving points of law of general public importance. On average it hears about 40 cases a year but in 1965 it heard 53 cases; the majority of these will be civil cases often on abstruse points of law involving company taxation, death duties and stamp duties where large amounts of money are at stake. It is necessary to have permission, known as leave, to appeal to the House of Lords: this leave in civil cases must be obtained either from the Court of Appeal (Civil Division) or from the House of Lords itself, in which case it is given by a special committee.

(ii) *The judges.*—The "judges" who sit in the House of Lords are specially created Life Peers so that technically they are full members of the House of Lords and as such they occasionally take part in debates although it is acknowledged that their real role is as "judges". They are commonly called the Law Lords, but formally their title is Lords of Appeal In Ordinary appointed by the Queen on the advice of the Prime Minister under the Appellate Jurisdiction Act 1876. The maximum number is nine and they must have had at least fifteen years' experience as a barrister or two years as a puisne judge before appointment. In practice appointments are rarely made before the age of sixty by which time the experience is likely to be more like thirty-five years. One judge from Scotland and one from Northern Ireland are appointed since the House of Lords hears certain appeals from these countries. The salary is £11,250 per annum. Appointments are generally by promotion from the Court of Appeal. The president of the court is the Lord Chancellor although he himself takes part infrequently.

It is usual for five judges to sit to hear a case and for a majority verdict to be given by way of individual decisions (technically called "speeches" or "opinions"). By the use of certain *ex-officio* judges, for example ex-Lord Chancellors, the Lord Chief Justice and the Master of the Rolls, it is just possible for the court to sit in two divisions. The court always reserves judgment and this means that there is often a delay of two months or more before the individual speeches are available. The House of Lords in its legislative capacity then by order gives effect to the finding of the court. This shows that the House of Lords in its judicial capacity is no more than a committee of the House of Lords in its legislative capacity.

(g) The Judicial Committee of the Privy Council

This committee of the Privy Council has long been charged with the responsibility for "advising" Her Majesty on appeal cases brought to the monarch as the final appeal court, in matters civil and criminal, from the overseas possessions of the Crown. The "advice" is always taken and effect is given to it by an order in council.

The committee consists of a number of Law Lords; the quorum is three but five may sit. In view of the standing of these judges very considerable store is placed on the "advice" given, even though the decisions are persuasive only and not binding on the English courts. Occasionally a judge from the colony concerned will be invited to attend and assist the committee. The rule used to be that apparently unanimous "advice" was given, but now the judges are free to express dissenting views if they wish.

The jurisdiction of the committee has been affected by the attainment of independence by so many ex-colonies and this can be seen in that in 1937 122 appeals were heard whereas in 1965 the number of cases heard was only 39. The committee has also jurisdiction to hear appeals from ecclesiastical courts and from the disciplinary findings of certain domestic tribunals such as those concerned with the professional conduct of doctors, dentists and opticians.

3 THE ORGANISATION AND JURISDICTION OF THE CRIMINAL COURTS

Diagram of the organisation of the Criminal Court Structure

1. Summary Offences

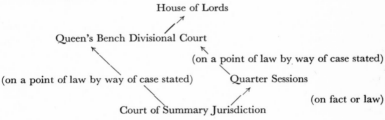

House of Lords

Queen's Bench Divisional Court

(on a point of law by way of case stated)

(on a point of law by way of case stated)   Quarter Sessions

(on fact or law)

Court of Summary Jurisdiction

2. Indictable Offences

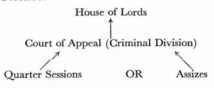

House of Lords

Court of Appeal (Criminal Division)

Quarter Sessions   OR   Assizes

(on prosecution showing prima facie case the case is committed for trial to)

Examining Magistrates holding Preliminary Enquiry (Committal Proceedings)

N.B. The arrows represent the possible course of an appeal.

(a) The magistrates

(i) *Their jurisdiction.*—All criminal cases are begun before magistrates. Those offences which are very trivial are dealt with in their court of summary jurisdiction, also known historically as petty sessions. Cases, for example, of careless and dangerous driving, shoplifting and being drunk and disorderly are all heard there. Such crimes are called summary offences and are tried by the bench of magistrates addressed as "Your Worships" and sitting always without a jury. This court will consist of from two to seven magistrates and collectively they will hear the prosecution and the defence case, then decide whether or not the case has been proved to their satisfaction and convict or acquit the accused person accordingly. If they convict the accused they will then pronounce sentence. Where children and young persons are involved they attend before a juvenile court. There are limits to the punishment the magistrates can impose: six months' imprisonment for one offence and/or £100 fine, or twelve months' imprisonment for two or more offences. Appeal generally is to quarter sessions but appeal on a point of law is, by way of case stated, to the Queens' Bench Divisional Court and possibly to the House of Lords.

Those offences which are regarded as of a more serious nature are called indictable offences and here the procedure is quite different. In such cases one or two magistrates sit as examining magistrates to hear in full the prosecution case, and, having heard it, he or they have to decide whether or not it warrants putting the accused person on trial. This process is intended to ensure that the prosecution case is prepared and presented fully and without delay. The magistrates do not try the case, they are only concerned to see whether or not the prosecution have made out a *prima facie* case against the accused. If they do not think so, then they discharge the accused; but there is nothing to stop the prosecution returning with fresh evidence at a later date and asking the examining justices to re-hear the matter and then send the accused for trial. Generally the examining magistrates do commit the accused for trial because the prosecution is careful only to pursue a matter where they have sufficient evidence to make a case. The accused person is committed for trial either to quarter sessions or to assizes. These proceedings are sometimes called "a preliminary enquiry" or "committal proceedings".

(ii) *The appointment of magistrates.*—Magistrates, or as the older title has it, Justices of the Peace, are local citizens appointed by the Monarch to the commission of the peace for the area in which they live. They receive no salary and they are not trained lawyers. The office is of great antiquity but today they are of vital significance in the criminal court system and there are some 16,000 of them. Magistrates are recommended for appointment by local advisory committees: they are required to be persons held in respect in their locality and capable of exercising sound judgment. Often they are well-known in public life prior to appointment and in many instances they have been prominent in some political organisation. The selection process being secret is highly controversial. On appointment some limited training in the duties of a magistrate is given, but the lack of legal knowledge is in theory compensated for by the requirement that each bench of magistrates must have a clerk, who is a lawyer, and who can thus assist them with legal advice where necessary.

(iii) *Stipendiary magistrates.*—Lay magistrates must be distinguished from stipendiary magistrates and, in London, Metropolitan magistrates, who are full-time salaried lawyers carrying out the work of magistrates in their area. Comparatively few cities have chosen to have stipendiary magistrates, but whether on the grounds of expense or through satisfaction with the existing system is not clear.

(b) Quarter Sessions

(i) *Function.*—Quarter Sessions has two main functions. One is to hear appeals from the decisions of magistrates given in their court of summary jurisdiction: the other is to try, with a jury, indictable offences where the examining magistrates have committed the accused for trial. The jurisdiction of quarter sessions in relation to indictable offences is to try "all manner of crimes" except those which have been specifically reserved to assizes.

In its appeal capacity the court treats the matter as a re-hearing but it does not use a jury: its decision on fact is final but on a point of law the Queen's Bench Divisional Court will consider a case stated. It is only on a "not guilty" plea to an indictable offence that a jury is invariably sworn.

(ii) *Composition.*—The composition of quarter sessions varies as between a county and a borough. In a county there is a legally qualified chairman who sits with from two to nine magistrates. In practice the chairman forms the court; often he is a judge or a retired judge and in any event he must be legally qualified. He receives a salary. In a borough there is a Recorder, who is a practising barrister, specially appointed by the Crown to do the quarter sessions' work on a paid part-time basis. There are approximately ninety-six Recorders and it is frequently from their ranks that the appointment to a High Court judgeship is made.

Quarter sessions is a court with a long history. It takes its name from the requirement in 1363 that it should meet four times a year. Pressure of business means that it now meets at least four times a year.

(iii) *Appeals.*—Appeal from a conviction and/or sentence at quarter sessions dealing with an indictable offence in its original jurisdiction is to the Court of Appeal (Criminal Division). Appeal from the decision of quarter sessions in its appellate capacity on fact is not possible; however on a point of law it is possible for a case to be stated for the consideration of the Queen's Bench Divisional Court.

(c) Assizes

(i) *Origins and background.*—The criminal court to which the most serious criminal cases are sent for trial is the assizes. This is a local court which has a very long history going back to the days when the King sent his judges around the country to the major towns to act as his deputies in maintaining law and order. Hence today the assize judge is treated with great respect and much pageantry is attached to his visit. There are seven assize circuits having the mundane titles of Northern, Western, Midland, South-Eastern, North-Eastern, Oxford and Wales and Chester. Within each circuit there are a number of assize towns, frequently the ancient county towns, and three times a year one or more judges of the Queen's Bench Division will visit these towns to deal with all the most serious offences with which persons have been charged in the locality since the last assizes. The age old commissions given to the mediaeval judges, the commissions of the peace, of oyer and terminer and of gaol delivery are still used today. A Royal Commission under the chairmanship of Lord Beeching is at present examining the arrangements for assizes and quarter sessions.

(ii) *Jurisdiction.*—The cases which are heard at assizes include murder (and all forms of homicide), very serious offences against the person, substantial theft, complicated cases of fraud, perjury, forgery and bigamy. The division of work with the quarter sessions, is, however, not absolutely clear-cut.

Trial of a "not guilty" plea is by judge and jury: the jury decide on guilt and the judge, if it is necessary, on sentence. "Guilty" pleas are dealt with by sentence by the judge alone.

Appeal from conviction and/or sentence at assizes is with leave to the Court of Appeal (Criminal Division).

(iii) *The Old Bailey and Crown courts.*—It will be noticed that London is not an assize circuit. Instead, since 1834, it has had the Central Criminal Court, better known as The Old Bailey, to deal with, in general terms, all indictable offence cases in the London area. This court is in almost continuous session and sits usually in four divisions. A Queen's Bench Division judge is frequently assigned to the Central Criminal Court to take the most serious cases.

On a similar basis, courts, known as Crown courts, have been established since 1956 in Liverpool and Manchester. In each city a full-time judge, known as the Recorder, sitting continuously, deals with both quarter sessions and assize business. Again a Queen's Bench Division judge will visit the Crown courts to try the most serious cases.

(d) Queen's Bench Divisional Court

(i) *Appellate jurisdiction.*—This court, which consists of the Lord Chief Justice and two Queen's Bench Division judges, or alternatively three Queen's Bench Division judges, hears in its criminal capacity appeals from the magistrates in summary cases on a point of law "by way of case stated". The process involves the lower court in preparing a summary of the point of law concerned, *i.e.* a case stated in writing, and explaining the reasoning which it applied in coming to its conclusion. One very unusual feature is that the prosecutor as well as the defendant can appeal to this court "by way of case stated". The divisional court will then hear argument on the point of law concerned and give judgment. Appeal from its decision is, with leave, to the House of Lords and here again the prosecutor can appeal if he has been unsuccessful before the divisional court. This is quite exceptional in that normally there is no appeal from an acquittal but the prosecutor's right here is limited to raising a point of law. He cannot appeal on fact.

(ii) *Supervisory jurisdiction.*—In addition to this appeal function, the divisional court also supervises the activities of the lower courts and is specially concerned with the freedom of the individual. Hence it controls the issue of the writ of *habeas corpus* and the orders of *certiorari*, *mandamus* and prohibition. This supervisory jurisdiction is of very considerable importance and is fully examined in chapter 5.

(e) Court of Appeal (Criminal Division)

On the 1st October 1966 the Court of Criminal Appeal was abolished and its jurisdiction was transferred to the Court of Appeal. The reasons for the change were to meet the criticism that the three Queen's Bench Division judges who made up the Court of Criminal Appeal had a built-in bias in favour of their brother judges' conduct of the trial at assizes: and also that the large number of judges taking part in the work of the court led to inconsistency, particularly in sentencing.

The new court is to consist of three judges, the Lord Chief Justice, one Lord Justice of Appeal and one Queen's Bench Division judge.

If the Lord Chief Justice, who is the President of this division, is not available, a Lord Justice of Appeal or a Queen's Bench Division judge may take his place. The Queen's Bench Division judges will be specially selected by the Lord Chief Justice.

Appeal cases will come to this court from quarter sessions in its original jurisdiction and from assizes; and also from the Central Criminal Court and Crown courts. Appeal may be against conviction and/or sentence.

The 1966 Criminal Appeal Act making the new arrangement also gives the court wide discretion in dealing with appeals. It may quash a conviction wherever it considers it "unsafe or unsatisfactory" to allow it to stand; but the court retains the right to permit a technical point to succeed on appeal yet allow the conviction to stand. Appeal is, with leave, to the House of Lords.

(f) House of Lords

The House of Lords in its judicial capacity is the supreme court of appeal in criminal as in civil cases. Leave is necessary before an appeal will be heard and very few criminal cases actually reach the House of Lords. Those that do, concern a point of law deemed to be of general public importance: because of this it is possible for the prosecutor as well as the defendant to appeal. Cases can come either from the Court of Appeal (Criminal Division) or from the Queen's Bench Divisional Court.

4 THE PROCEDURE OF THE COURT—CIVIL

A civil case is always an unresolved dispute between two or more parties. The parties may be natural persons or one or both may be corporations, i.e. an artificial legal person such as a limited company or a local authority. The party bringing the case is called the plaintiff and the party against whom it is brought is called the defendant. In a civil case then, the plaintiff sues the defendant.

A very important aspect of the law is the procedure which the courts lay down that the parties must follow in order to bring the case at all. It would clearly be a waste of time for the judge to have to hear a case in which no preparations at all had been made and neither party had any idea of what the other party intended to prove. This would result in much repetition leading to frequent requests for adjournments and cases would drag on endlessly. To avoid this state of affairs the courts have long since laid down detailed rules which govern the way in which an action can be brought.

The object of this law of procedure is to save the time of the court and consequently the expense to the parties by analysing in detail the matters in dispute between them. If the procedure is successful the judge can see from the necessary documents, before he reaches the court, exactly what is the plaintiff's case and exactly where the plaintiff and the defendant are not able to agree. These documents used throughout the pre-trial stages are known collectively as "the pleadings".

(a) The Pleadings

The High Court is the place where pleadings are the rule. The county court has a set procedure by way of forms but this tends to reflect the comparatively straightforward and limited nature of that court's work.

Generally in High Court actions the plaintiff starts by issuing a writ against the defendant. This writ, which is formally authenticated by the court, notifies the defendant that an action is to be brought against him and an accompanying statement of claim, prepared by the plaintiff, sets out in full detail the grounds and the substance of the claim.

The defendant must enter an appearance to the writ and, following the delivery of the statement of claim, he must reply to this statement in full, in documentary form, submitting his defence. Although in theory the defence has to be submitted in 14 days, in practice the whole course of the pleadings frequently takes months. This is largely because the statement of claim and the defence are technical documents which almost always have to be prepared by counsel. One significant factor which will indicate the need for caution here is that any failure to deny a charge made in the statement of claim will be taken by the court to be an admission of its truth. Hence a defence will have to be most detailed in its denials. Sometimes advantage can be gained by requesting further and better particulars of the statement of claim or the defence as the case may be.

Depending on the facts it may be possible for the defendant to accompany his defence with a set-off or counter claim to which, in turn, the plaintiff will be called upon to submit a defence.

Other documents which may be introduced and which then form part of the pleadings are a reply, a rejoinder, a surrejoinder, a rebutter and a surrebutter: but such documents are exceptional in a case.

(b) The trial

When ultimately the pleadings are complete the case is ready for trial with the issues between the parties clarified. The majority of trials in civil cases in the High Court are heard by a judge sitting alone. It is possible to have a jury in certain cases, particularly libel and slander, and where this is so the judge deals with matters of law and the jury with matters of fact. However jury cases are not common.

The judge hears counsel—this is the usual case but a party can represent himself if he wishes—on both sides, hears the parties and their witnesses and when all has been said he gives his decision, called judgment, in the light of the facts as he applies them to the principles of law involved. Sometimes the case turns entirely on fact— in a factory accident the judge may have to decide whether or not the employer's system of work was a safe system; in a car accident he may have to decide which driver was negligent and to what extent; at other times the judge may be much more concerned with law and in particular with the doctrine of judicial precedent under which he has to relate the previously declared principles of law to the facts before him. At the last the judge gives judgment and he will then award damages, or other remedy asked for, in accordance with his findings and also decide how the costs of the action shall be borne.

Should a case go to appeal the party appealing is called "the appellant" and the other party is called "the respondent". If a further appeal follows, the same terms are used, so it is possible for the respondent in the Court of Appeal to become the appellant in the House of Lords!

5 THE PROCEDURE OF THE COURT—CRIMINAL

The contrast between civil and criminal procedure is considerable. In place of the slow documentary niceties of a civil case the criminal process is quicker and almost non-documentary in nature. Here a man's freedom is at stake and as such the law brooks little delay.

(a) On arrest

The moment an arrest is made rules must be observed which lead to three fundamental rights on the part of the accused person. First he must at once be informed what crime he is alleged to have committed: second he must not thereafter be subjected to any pressures, physical or mental, to obtain information from him and third he must, following arrest, be brought before a magistrate within twenty-four hours (excluding Sunday) and the magistrate must decide whether or not to remand him in custody or grant bail.

(b) **Summary offences**

(i) *The trial.*—In summary offences it is not often that an arrest is made. Instead the defendant will normally receive a summons to a hearing of the court. If he pleads "not guilty" the procedure in court will be a statement by the prosecutor outlining the facts which it is alleged show that the defendant has committed an offence, followed by the evidence of the prosecution witnesses. The defendant may then submit that the prosecution have not made out a case against him and that therefore he should be discharged— this is called a submission that there is no case to answer. As an alternative he may proceed to rebut the prosecution case by calling the defence witnesses and explaining in full the defence to the charge. The magistrates normally retire to consider the case and then return either to convict and sentence the defendant or to acquit and discharge him. In a great many cases notably Road Traffic Act offences, the defendant pleads "guilty" and arrangements have been made in certain cases, for such persons to plead guilty by post, so doing away with the need for attendance.

There are all sorts of minor variations on the procedure of the court: for example, if the offence charged is one for which a sentence of three months' imprisonment is possible then the defendant can choose to stand trial at quarter sessions before a jury rather than undergo summary trial before the magistrates: again when the magistrates have convicted the defendant and before sentencing him they hear his record (or antecedents), if this record is very bad and they think he deserves a greater punishment than they can inflict, they may send the defendant to quarter sessions for that court to sentence him: a further qualification to what has been said is that certain indictable offences can be tried summarily if the parties so consent.

(ii) *Appeals.*—An appeal from conviction and/or sentence by the court of summary jurisdiction is generally to quarter sessions where a rehearing takes place. The witnesses all appear and the court forms its own view. There is no further appeal on fact from quarter sessions. On a point of law there is an appeal from the court of summary jurisdiction or from the quarter sessions by way of a process known as "a case stated". The unsuccessful party, prosecutor or defendant,

may ask the lower court to state a case in writing for the consideration of the Queen's Bench Divisional Court. This case, which will
be prepared by the clerk of the court, will set out the point of law
involved and explain the reasoning applied by the magistrates.
The divisional court will duly hear arguments about the point of
law, and give judgment. They will either confirm the view taken by
the lower court or differ from it and send the case back to the
magistrates for them to deal with again in the light of the divisional
court's decision. Although the prosecutor can here appeal on a
point of law this is exceptional and the general rule is that there is
no appeal from an acquittal before the magistrates, or for that
matter from an acquittal before quarter sessions or assizes.

(c) Indictable offences

(i) *Preliminary enquiry.*—Turning now from summary to indictable
offences the process in an Indictable case starts with the preliminary
enquiry into the prosecution case by the examining magistrates.
The prosecution presents its case in full and the statements of the
witnesses are taken down by the clerk of the court and signed by
the witnesses. These statements are called depositions because they
are made on oath. This makes for a slow process but it does give the
defence the opportunity of hearing all the prosecution case and
therefore knowing exactly what case it will have to meet at the trial.
In most cases counsel for the accused at the preliminary enquiry
"reserves his defence".

(ii) *Trial at quarter sessions or assizes.*—At the trial at quarter
sessions or at assizes the indictment will be read by the clerk of
the court to the accused and he will be required to plead either
guilty or not guilty. This is called the arraignment. If the plea is
guilty, the prosecutor outlines the circumstances of the offence
and the defence counsel will make a plea in mitigation. The judge
having heard the record of the accused and what has been said on
his behalf will then sentence him. If, on the other hand, the plea is
"not guilty" a jury of twelve is empanelled and the case proceeds.
The prosecution counsel opens the case and then calls his witnesses;
counsel for the defence follows with an explanation of the defence
case and then calls the defendant (not invariably) and other defence
witnesses. The judge ultimately "sums up" the case for the benefit
of the jury, a process which involves summarising the main issues
and explaining the law in relation to those issues. Then the jury
retire to arrive in secret at their verdict. They are required to be
convinced that the prosecution has proved the guilt of the accused

beyond all reasonable doubt and if they are so convinced then they will find the accused "guilty". If they are not so convinced then they must find the accused "not guilty". Formerly the verdict had to be unanimous, but under the Criminal Justice Act 1967 a majority verdict with not more than two in the minority is to be accepted. Following conviction a plea in mitigation will be made and then sentence will be pronounced.

(iii) *Appeals.*—An appeal against conviction and/or sentence lies to the Court of Appeal (Criminal Division) and here the three judges will limit themselves to the actual points of appeal raised on behalf of the defence. This hearing is not a retrial and no jury is required. Not unnaturally the court is unwilling to upset the verdict of the jury but they have power to quash a conviction for proper cause or in certain circumstances to order a retrial. Both powers are sparingly used. The court may permit a technical point of an appeal to succeed but still allow the sentence to stand if they feel that no miscarriage of justice has taken place.

A final appeal on the application of the prosecutor or defendant is, with leave, possible to the House of Lords but in practice such appeals, in criminal cases, are rare. When they do occur it is usually a highly technical point of law which is involved.

6 THE DECISION OF THE COURT—IN A CIVIL CASE

In a civil case the decision of the court is almost always the decision of the judge and since in most of its civil branches the law has been built up on the basis of previously decided cases or precedents, every new decision adds something to, confirms, or qualifies the existing legal principles in that field. Such a system pre-supposes that counsel for the parties, and the judge, know the principles involved but that the particular case in question has certain facets which make it arguable how those principles should be applied. It is the task of counsel to present the relevant precedents to the judge and to argue before him the interpretation which should be placed on them so as to result in the case being decided in favour of the plaintiff or the defendant respectively, but in conformity always with the existing principles of law.

(a) Judicial precedents

The emphasis which has come to be placed on precedents has led as has been seen (see chapter 1. Sources: case law) to the formation of a doctrine of judicial precedent. This doctrine arises from the reasoning that more weight ought to be attached to the decisions, *i.e.* precedents, of the senior courts than to those of single judges in the lower courts. Today, however, less emphasis is placed on the status of the court giving the decision and more attention is given to the reasoning of the judge: and a recent announcement indicates that the House of Lords will no longer regard itself as necessarily bound by its previous decisions.

In practice nonetheless the most striking feature of a visit to a civil appeal court is the emphasis on precedents and the argument about the interpretation of each precedent in relation to the particular facts under consideration. Each of the Law Lords, for instance, has in the court his own bookcase of volumes from which counsel are proposing to quote in the course of the case. The result is that when each judge gives his judgment in the case, much of what he says will be concerned with explaining his view of the principles of law involved and their connection with the precedents quoted. If the court agrees with the reasoning it is said to "follow" the precedent: if it does not find that the precedent is exactly applicable to the situation it is said to "distinguish" it: if it decides that the reasoning in it was faulty it is said to "over-rule" it.

(b) Difficulties

Superficially it appears a somewhat simple matter to decide whether a precedent is in point or not, but in practice the law has so developed over the centuries that a case brought today is almost certain to be concerned with some refinement of a well-established principle. There are exceptions, of course, where some new development sets a special problem. For example in *Bridlington Relay Ltd.* v. *Yorkshire Electricity Board* (1965) the court was required to determine whether or not the right to receive a television signal was a legal right protected by the law relating to Nuisance. In the result the court held that it was not: but there was clearly little available in the way of precedent to assist the court. It was necessarily making new law.

Sometimes the court is presented with a wide range of precedents from which it must endeavour to extract the legal principle to be applied to the case before it. The House of Lords, in *Wheat* v. *E. Lacon & Co., Ltd.* (1966) a case concerned with an occupier's liability for dangerous premises, was asked to consider thirty-three precedents.

On the other hand sometimes there is a dearth of precedents. In

Tucker v. *Farm and General Investment Trust, Ltd.* (1966) the question to be decided was who owned the lambs produced by sheep which were the subject of a hire-purchase agreement. Generally the ownership of goods under a hire purchase agreement remains with the party selling until the goods are paid for. Hence the sheep belonged to the Trust. The Court of Appeal in this situation, however, had no difficulty in deciding that the farmer was entitled to the lambs, but to find a precedent to follow the court had to go back to 1586 and the case of *Wood* v. *Ash and Foster.*

7 THE DECISION OF THE COURT—IN A CRIMINAL CASE

(a) The verdict

In criminal cases of consequence, assuming that the accused has pleaded "not guilty", the decision of the court rests with the jury. At the conclusion of the judge's summing up of the case the twelve men and women who make up the jury retire to be locked in the jury room to arrive in secret at their verdict. On their return to court the foreman of the jury announces their verdict on each count of the indictment against the accused. If the verdict is "not guilty" then the judge will order the discharge of the accused and he is free to leave the court without a stain on his character. Nor may be he tried again for that offence on the same set of circumstances. If, however, the verdict is "guilty" then the judge assumes the responsibility of sentencing "the prisoner" as the accused now becomes. His criminal record, if he has one, is first presented to the court and in the light of this and of what the prisoner or his counsel may say in mitigation, the judge then pronounces sentence.

In criminal cases of lesser significance those which are tried before magistrates, there is no jury. The court therefore assumes the function of the jury. It hears the prosecution case and then the defence case and decides whether or not to convict the accused. If the court convicts, it then proceeds to sentence within its rather limited powers. If the court feels that the prisoner deserves a more severe punishment than it can inflict, it will commit the prisoner to quarter sessions for sentence.

(b) Appeals

Most criminal cases turn on a matter of fact; for example, whether the accused person committed the act in question or not. It is only occasionally that a case arises which involves an argument on a point of law. From the Magistrates it is possible to appeal in such cases to the Queen's Bench Divisional Court.

An example of such a case is *Hall* v. *Hyder* (1966). A licensee, who had been charged before the magistrates with supplying intoxicating liquor to a person under the age of eighteen, pleaded "not guilty" on the grounds that the drink supplied was "shandy" which was not "intoxicating liquor". The magistrates dismissed the case. On appeal by the prosecutor by case stated to the Queen's Bench Divisional Court, the Lord Chief Justice, Lord PARKER, explained the unanimous view of the court in this way: "In my judgment the justices here came to a wrong conclusion and I base my judgment on a very short ground . . . what the publican does when he sells shandy is to sell beer and separately either lemonade or ginger beer and then as agent for the purchaser and as agent only, pours one into the other." There was thus a sale of beer, which is an intoxicating liquor. The case was remitted to the magistrates to continue the hearing.

A further appeal, if the point of law is deemed to be of general public importance, lies to the House of Lords.

From the original criminal jurisdiction of quarter sessions and assizes appeal lies to the Court of Appeal (Criminal Division) and thereafter with leave to the House of Lords. Most appeals are against the sentence of the court, some concern the judge's summing up or some other alleged fault in the conduct of the trial and a few turn on aspects of criminal law.

An example of the latter is *Button* v. *Director of Public Prosecutions* (1966) which went to the House of Lords on the highly technical point of whether or not the crime of causing an affray could properly be charged when the outbreak of violence had occurred on private premises, a dance hall, as opposed to in a public place. The Lord Chancellor, giving the judgment of the court, made an exhaustive survey of the criminal law authorities and ultimately ruled that the offence of causing an affray could take place on private premises.

Chapter 4

The Making of Law by the Administration

1 THE ADMINISTRATION—DEFINITION

The preceding chapters have examined the way in which Parliament makes law and the way in which the courts make law. It is now necessary to consider the way in which law is made by the administration.

If this book had been written one hundred years ago this chapter would not have been necessary because all the law that was made would have fallen within the two chapters referred to. It is only in the last hundred years that this rather strange body, the administration, has come to play what is now so large a part in the making of law in this country. The development has occurred because of the rapid change in the accepted role of the State. Whereas a hundred years ago the State was expected to provide law and order and generally leave the way clear for private enterprise, today the State is required to intervene in and provide throughout life a whole range of services for the public welfare. From a National Insurance and a National Health Scheme the demands have developed so that at the present time the State is concerned even to regulate prices and incomes and to provide employment—matters once taken to be the stronghold of the private enterprise system.

This change in the role of the State has meant that Parliament has come to play a much larger part in affairs and in the creation of these public services by legislation. In order to provide these same services Parliament has frequently found it essential to permit the details to be filled in by means of delegated legislation and for the actual practical working of the scheme to be carried out by other bodies. These "other bodies" are what is meant by the term "the administration". This chapter will be concerned to look at the part played by some of these other bodies. Legislation and delegated legislation were considered in chapter 2. This chapter is concerned with the implementation of legislation and with the law which the administration makes in so doing.

95

(a) Administrative bodies

Among the bodies which fall within the term, the administration, are:

(i) *The central government departments.*—"Whitehall" as it is often called. The Ministers of the Government in charge of each department are very important figures in the administration. By legislation many of them are charged with particular responsibilities which amount to the making of law; to take one example, in many matters affecting education, the Minister of Education is made the sole judge and his decisions can rarely be challenged.

(ii) *Local authorities in England and Wales.*—They consist of elected members and they number: county councils 58, county borough councils 80, non-county borough councils 270, urban district councils 535, and rural district councils 473. There is as well a nation-wide system of parish government, and at the other extreme there is London Government which consists of the Greater London Council, 32 London boroughs and the Corporation of the City of London.

(iii) *Public corporations.*—These are artificial legal bodies set up to provide a particular service such as Electricity or the Port of London or Air Transport. Normally under the creating statute these corporations will be given wide powers to carry on the service in question.

(iv) *Administrative tribunals.*—These are established directly by Act of Parliament to come to a judicial decision in matters of conflict between the individual and the administration or even between individuals where the State has intervened in the relationship.

(b) Important role

It will be obvious from this list that "the administration" plays an important part in the lives of everyone in this country, and that the law which it makes affects every citizen directly. The imposition of the 70 miles per hour speed limit is made law by a statutory instrument issued by the Minister of Transport and is thus law made by the administration. The rent which a landlord may charge a tenant for the use of his property may well be fixed by a rent tribunal or a rent assessment committee—by the administration. The pension to which a disabled serviceman is entitled is decided by a Pensions Appeal Tribunal—by the administration. The use to which land can be put is subject to permission being obtained from a local authority or, following an appeal, from the Minister of Housing and Local

Government—by the administration. All these decisions are to the man-in-the-street "the law" in the matter, just as much as if the ruling had come from the Lord Chief Justice himself. It would certainly be possible to argue that administrative law today more nearly affects the citizen than does any other branch of law.

In this chapter a brief survey will be made of the work of the administrative bodies set out above and of the law which they make. Delegated legislation has already been considered in chapter 2 and it can be shortly disposed of, although it must not be overlooked that the law which is made in this way by central Government Ministers and local authorities is a very important aspect of the law made by the administration. Following delegated legislation the emphasis will be on administrative tribunals and the work which they do, and on administrative inquiries and the part which they play, in the law making decisions of the administration. Later in the chapter it will be necessary to consider the legal standing of these tribunals and inquiries as a result of the Franks Committee Report 1957 and the legislation which followed it. Finally the controversial modern use of compulsory purchase powers will be considered separately since, from the point of view of the man-in-the-street, this topic is of major significance as an example of law-making by the administration.

2   THE ADMINISTRATION—LEGISLATIVE POWERS

Beyond question one of the most important aspects of administrative law is the power to make law which Parliament has delegated to central Government Ministers, local authorities and public corporations. The whole subject of delegated legislation has been fully considered in chapter 2 where various examples were given of actual statutory instruments which have been issued by Ministers under statutory authority.

(a) Ministers' powers

At this point it is only necessary to emphasise the enormous scope of these powers which have been delegated to the various Government Ministers. In the field of education for instance the Minister for Education and Science has been authorised to produce statutory instruments to give effect to the policy of his department throughout the range of matters with which he is concerned. One can thus envisage the sort of statutory instruments involved—school milk and school meals: grants for students: school buildings and fittings:

appointment and dismissal of staff: curricula: school health service: and training of teachers. To take another aspect of government, transport; the Minister of Transport has been given extensive power to produce statutory instruments for many matters falling within that department's responsibility. An outstanding example of such an instrument is Statutory Instrument 1288/66 called the Motor Vehicles (Construction and Use) Regulations which runs to 113 pages and lays down in detail the standards which must be observed both in the manufacture of a motor vehicle and in the maintenance of such a vehicle thereafter. Other examples of statutory instruments made by the Minister of Transport are that laying down the 70 miles per hour speed limit and those which lay down in great detail the road traffic signs which motorists must obey. The warning sign which the "lollipop" man carries at a children's crossing, for example, has to be a specified size and colour and even the letters of the wording have to be a particular height: and this is also true of all mandatory road traffic signs and devices. It is thus a good defence for a motorist accused of failing to comply with such a sign to show that the sign in question does not comply with the statutory instrument.

(b) Ministers' influence

In addition to the law which Ministers make by statutory instrument there is also to be considered the very powerful influence which Ministers have over local authorities and also over public corporations. The apparent legislative power of local authorities to make by-laws was seen in the course of chapter 2 to be largely illusory. Since the proposed by-laws must have the confirmation of the appropriate Minister it follows that basically this law-making power also lies in the hands of the Minister. An equally effective method by which a central Government Minister can influence local authorities is by the use of the ministry circular. Although such a circular is not law-making it contains the views of the Minister on what he takes to be the law; and within local authorities these views are accorded such respect that they often come to be treated as if they were the law! Appendix A contains an example of a ministry circular. There are other methods also by which a Minister can hold in check the activities of local authorities; for example, he may send inspectors to examine any local service, and in particular the district auditor will annually check the accounts of (most) local authorities; the Minister may in some circumstances order the taking over of a particular service as a default power; or he may threaten to withhold Government grant if his wishes are not complied with.

Thus the power of local authorities to make law is very closely restricted; so much so that for all practical purposes there is no such power available to a local authority.

With public corporations the position is rather different in that some very restricted power to make law for its own purposes is given to the particular body by the Act of Parliament which creates it. The power of British Railways to make it a prosecutable offence to pull the communication cord without good cause, or to travel on the railway without intending to pay the fare, are typical examples. These and like matters are legislative powers put to use by a public corporation under the authority of an Act of Parliament.

3 ADMINISTRATIVE TRIBUNALS—NATURE AND FUNCTIONS

One particular type of administrative body which has proved itself to be of great value is the tribunal. A tribunal is a kind of court which is set up by an Act of Parliament to hear and determine certain disputes. In many cases the dispute is between a central Government department and the ordinary citizen: one such example is the amount of unemployment benefit a person is entitled to under the relevant legislation. In other cases the dispute may be between one citizen and another in a matter where Parliament has intervened with legislation to regulate their relationship. Such, for example, as a dispute over what is a fair rent for certain property where a landlord and a tenant do not agree.

In these cases and in many others like them Parliament has foreseen that disputes will inevitably arise and has provided that a court-like body shall be available to determine the matter. These bodies established under the various Acts of Parliament are known as administrative tribunals. Below in summary form details are given of the composition and jurisdiction of the more important of these tribunals. It will be seen that there is little in common between the tribunals either in composition or in jurisdiction: the only common factor is their establishment by Act of Parliament.

(a) Social Security Tribunals

(i) *National Insurance Tribunals*

Act of Parliament   National Insurance Act 1946.

Composition	Chairman and two members. Chairman almost always a lawyer selected by the Minister of Social Security from a list kept by the Lord Chancellor. He receives remuneration. The members are selected by the Minister from two panels, one of persons representing employers and the other of persons representing employees.
Number	There are in England and Wale some 173 local National Insurances Tribunals and 29 in Scotland. Cases are referred to them where the decision of a local insurance officer is contested. In 1965 the tribunals heard some 30,500 cases and the National Insurance Commissioner and his deputies heard some 1,600 cases on appeal. The appeal decisions are reported and a body of case law is being built up.
Appeal	Appeal from the tribunal is to the National Insurance Commissioner who is a full-time barrister of at least ten years' standing: or to one of his six full-time deputies.
Public Hearing	Yes.
Legal Representation	Yes.
Function	Disputes concerning unemployment benefit, sickness and death benefit, old age and widows' pensions, claims for family allowances.

(ii) *Industrial Injuries Appeal Tribunals*

Act of Parliament	National Insurance (Industrial Injuries) Act 1946.
Composition	As for the National Insurance Tribunal.
Number	173 as for the National Insurance Tribunal.
Appeal	To the Industrial Injuries Commissioner who is the same person as the National Insurance Commissioner and his deputies. 1965, 7,020 cases

	heard by tribunals and 989 by commissioners.
Public Hearing	Yes.
Legal Representation	Yes.
Function	To hear claims for benefit where claimant has suffered injury at work.

The Act also makes provision for the assessment of the degree of disability of a claimant. A medical board of two private practice doctors first assesses disability and then an appeal is possible to a Medical Appeal Tribunal which has a lawyer chairman assisted by two doctors. In 1965 there were 12 such tribunals and they dealt with 23,176 cases.

(iii) *Ministry of Social Security—Supplementary Benefits Commission Appeal Tribunals*

Act of Parliament	National Assistance Act 1948 as amended by the Ministry of Social Security Act 1966.
Composition	Chairman and two members. Chairman almost always a lawyer selected by the Ministry of Social Security from a list kept by the Lord Chancellor. The members are selected one by the Ministry and one by the National Assistance Board to represent work people from a list kept by the Minister.
Number	There are some 132 local appeal tribunals. Cases are referred to them where the decision of a local officer of the board is contested. In 1965 tribunals heard 9,582 cases.
Appeal	The tribunal's decision is final on fact but a point of law may be referred to the High Court.
Public Hearing	No.
Legal Representation	Yes.
Function	It hears disputes concerning the refusal of supplementary benefits or about the amount awarded.

(b) National Health Service Tribunals

Act of Parliament	National Health Service Act 1946.

There are several distinct kinds of tribunal. Local executive councils of which there are 134 being one for each local health authority. Each council will have a chairman and 20 members. The councils supervise the general medical, dental, pharmaceutical and opthalmic services provided under the Act. To do this they are required to appoint four local representative committees, one for each service, and these are responsible for advising the council. In particular the appropriate service committee will consider complaints against individual practitioners and then report to the council. Such committees will consist of a lay chairman and equal numbers of lay and professional people. In 1965 some 536 committees between them heard some 1,085 cases. Appeal is to the Minister of Health who will hold an inquiry before giving his decision.

There is also a National Health Service Tribunal with a lawyer-chairman appointed by the Lord Chancellor, and two members, one appointed by the Minister in consultation with the executive councils and one appointed by the Minister in consultation with the practitioners. The tribunal holds inquiries into whether or not a particular practitioner should be removed from the Health Service list of practitioners. An appeal by the practitioner concerned against the tribunal's finding lies to the Minister. In 1965 the tribunal heard only five cases.

As a result of the Mental Health Act 1959 some 15 Mental Health Review Tribunals, one for each regional hospital board area have been set up. The composition is of lawyers, doctors and other persons and the function is to review the detention of any person under the Act. In 1965 the tribunals heard some 1,150 applications.

(c) Lands Tribunal

Act of Parliament	Lands Tribunal Act 1949.
Composition	This tribunal has a barrister of at least seven years' standing as President and the other members usually four or five in number are appointed by the Lord Chancellor from lawyers and professionally qualified surveyors. One or more members sit to form a court.
Number	The tribunal may sit in London or in the provinces as occasion demands. In 1965 the tribunal heard 758 cases. The reasoned decisions given are frequently reported.

Appeal	Appeal lies to the Court of Appeal (Civil Division).
Public Hearing	Yes.
Legal Representation	Yes.
Function	The functions are:

    (i) to assess the value of land and/or premises on a compulsory acquisition or like dispute

    (ii) to assess the rateable value of land when the decision of a local valuation court as to the rateable value is disputed

    (iii) to hear and determine applications for the modification of restrictive covenants which affect the use of land.

(d) Rent Tribunals

Act of Parliament	Furnished Houses (Rent Control) Act 1946
Composition	These tribunals have a chairman and two members. The chairman will usually be drawn from the Lord Chancellor's list and the members are appointed by the Minister of Housing and Local Government from a wide field, but often from local government. The chairman and members receive payment for their services. There is also a full-time clerk and staff for each tribunal.
Number	There are 39 Rent Tribunals and in 1965 they heard 6,412 cases.
Appeal	There is no appeal from the tribunal on fact but there is a possible appeal to the High Court on a point of law.
Public Hearing	Yes.
Legal Representation	Yes.
Function	It determines a reasonable rent for the letting of certain furnished premises as between the landlord and the tenant.

N.B. Under the Rent Act 1965 Rent Assessment Committees have been set up to settle "a fair rent" between landlords and tenants of unfurnished property.

(e) Agricultural Land Tribunals

Act of Parliament	Agriculture Act 1947.
Composition	The three members of this tribunal are appointed by the Lord Chancellor. The chairman will be a lawyer of at least seven years' standing and of the two members, one will represent the interests of the farmers and the other will represent the interests of owners.
Number	There are eight tribunals one for each region and in 1965 they heard 141 cases.
Appeal	On a point of law appeal lies to the High Court.
Public Hearing	Yes.
Legal Representation	Yes.
Function	The tribunals decide whether or not to allow a notice to quit given to a tenant farmer to stand. This involves a consideration of the general principles of "good husbandry".

(f) Transport Tribunal

Act of Parliament	Transport Act 1962.
Composition	The tribunal consists of a chairman and four permanent members. The Chairman (called the President) is an experienced lawyer, and the other members are drawn from the worlds of transport (two) commerce and finance. The appointments are by the Crown on the recommendation of the Lord Chancellor and the Minister of Transport.
Number	There is only one tribunal and in 1965 it heard 63 cases.
Appeal	On a point of law appeal lies to the Court of Appeal (Civil Division).
Public Hearing	Yes.
Legal Representation	Yes.
Function	The tribunal sits in two divisions: one division deals with road and rail

passenger fares in the London area
and with charges for the carriage of
mail, the armed forces and the
police; the other division hears
appeals from the traffic commissioners' refusal of licences for goods
vehicles.

(g) Traffic Commissioners

Act of Parliament	Road Traffic Act 1960.
Composition	Three members form a court: the chairman is full-time, salaried and appointed by the Minister of Transport: the other members are selected by the Minister from two panels, one nominated by county councils and the other by boroughs and urban district councils.
Number	There are 10 traffic areas in England and Wales, each having traffic commissioners.
Appeal	Appeal generally lies to the Minister of Transport although this process has been criticised.
Public Hearing	Yes.
Legal Representation	Yes.
Function	The traffic commissioners grant or refuse licences to persons wishing to provide a public transport service and also for the vehicles, drivers and conductors concerned.

(h) Income Tax Appeal Tribunals

Individuals who wish to contest an assessment for Income Tax
can appeal to the General Commissioners of whom there are
some 5,500 divided into 631 areas. The persons appointed by
the Lord Chancellor are local business and professional men
with no special knowledge of taxation law, but they do have a
clerk to assist them.

For more complicated cases there are eight Special Commis-
sioners who are appointed by the Treasury and the Inland
Revenue department in roughly equal proportions. The
Treasury nominees will be barristers. All become full-time
Crown servants with national jurisdiction and they have no
further connection with the Inland Revenue department. The

Special Commissioners work in pairs on a circuit basis and in 1965 they heard 2,567 cases.

Appeal is to the High Court on a point of law.

The above examples of tribunals are not intended to be exhaustive and in fact it would be an unenviable task to attempt to produce a complete survey. The details concerning the tribunals and other bodies set out above are intended to drive home the point which has already been made that there is no real value in attempting to draw up any general principles about the composition and jurisdiction of tribunals. Each is created by a different Act of Parliament: the composition of each varies both in the qualification and in the selection: in the right of appeal and in the court or person to which the appeal is directed, there are obvious differences: and in function there is simply no likeness whatsoever.

(i) Increase of tribunals

The creation of tribunals continues apace. In 1965 (1) the Industrial Tribunal was set up under the Industrial Training Act 1964 to deal with appeals against assessment to levy under that Act and then later in the year it was given jurisdiction in claims under the Redundancy Payments Act 1965, and (2) the Plant Variety Rights Tribunal was set up under the Plant Varieties and Seeds Act 1964 to deal with cases concerning breaches of "copyright" in plants and seeds.

(j) Domestic tribunals

In addition to administrative tribunals there are other bodies sometimes called domestic tribunals which are of a quite different nature. A domestic tribunal has authority in matters of internal interest over the conduct of members of the particular organisation. The Law Society, for example, has substantial disciplinary powers over Solicitors: the General Medical Council has similar power over Doctors: trade unions exercise the vital right of expulsion over their members: these are clearly very important matters but they stem from internal agreement, from a willingness to subscribe to the rules. It is wise to regard these latter tribunals as quite different in nature from administrative tribunals although it must be admitted that these tribunals can reasonably be treated as falling within the subject public law. The right to exclude a man from following his trade or profession is indirectly of considerable consequence to the public and it is possible for the courts to intervene if such power is exercised other than strictly in accordance with the rules laid down.

(k) Special tribunals

A further word of warning concerning the word "tribunal" would not, at this point, be out of place. Care must also be exercised to distinguish administrative tribunals from bodies called tribunals which the Government may set up from time to time to investigate some particular matter. An example is the Aberfan Tribunal set up in 1966 to investigate the causes of the Aberfan disaster. Such a body is an "*ad hoc*" body, set up for the one particular purpose, and is not to be confused with an administrative tribunal.

(l) Procedure

There has long been controversy over the way in which administrative tribunals carry out their various tasks. Although they are "like courts" they are not courts and it was long ago decided that provided these tribunals comply with the rules of natural justice no objection will be upheld to their decisions on the grounds of their failure to act like a court.

By the term—the rules of natural justice—is meant two things. First, the tribunal must approach its task without obvious bias and second it must give an opportunity to both sides to state their case. In chapter 5 these principles will be considered in detail: at this point it is sufficient to note the dictum of Lord Chief Justice HEWART that "justice should not only be done but should manifestly and undoubtedly be seen to be done". This statement seems to be the test by which the judges control any such breach of the rules by a court or administrative tribunal.

In practice for many of the tribunals formal rules of procedure have been drawn up and issued as statutory instruments. These rules deal in detail with the way in which the hearing before the tribunal is to be conducted, and if the decision of the tribunal is to be allowed to stand they must be followed strictly.

(m) Question of independence

Another problem which arises in connection with tribunals is that they cannot have the same aura of independence which pertains to the work of a court. Whereas the doctrine of the independence of judiciary is well understood and applied in the present system of government, so far as administrative tribunals are concerned they are established by an Act of Parliament and are almost always placed under the wing of a central Government department. The Minister in charge of the Department may well be responsible for appointing the personnel of the tribunal and to some extent in supervising its work. It is consequently impossible for the tribunal to claim to be independent, although in fact most tribunals do operate in a way which is consistent with independence. This paradox is best explained in that in many instances the decisions which are being made are not of vital significance to the Ministry in question. Such matters as the exact amount of pension a claimant is entitled to, the rent of furnished accommodation, the grant of a licence to run a bus service, or the market value of land, are decisions which in themselves are of no express consequence to the Ministry. Thus the criticism that tribunals are too closely attached to the Ministries to be capable of truly impartial findings is a criticism which is superficial and does much less than justice to the true position.

(n) Diversity

The final point about administrative tribunals, which must always be borne in mind, is that it is dangerous to generalise. There are some 2,000 administrative tribunals in existence and the functions of these tribunals are as various as the personnel who compose them. It is consequently well nigh impossible to say that all tribunals display this or that characteristic; it is almost always necessary to particularise. Some for example, will hold public hearings, others will not: some encourage a party to be legally represented, others discourage it: some allow appeals on fact, others only allow appeals on a point of law and others again allow appeals on either fact or law or both: in some cases appeal is to a specially appointed appeal body such as the National Insurance Commissioner, whereas in other cases appeal is to a High Court judge (Income Tax Appeals) or to the Court of Appeal (Civil Division) (Lands Tribunal). Another and generally less acceptable alternative is an appeal to the appropriate Minister (Air Transport Licensing).

4   ADMINISTRATIVE INQUIRIES—NATURE AND FUNCTIONS

Besides the growth of administrative tribunals another form of administrative activity has increased enormously. This is the local inquiry. The advantage of an on the spot inquiry, to precede a minister's decision in a matter which Parliament has entrusted to the minister, is self-evident; and in the course of time it has become common practice for an Act of Parliament to require such an inquiry to be held. Because of this these inquiries are sometimes called "statutory inquiries".

The pattern followed is almost always along the following lines. Public notice is given of the proposed development. The minister is made aware of objections and he then, in turn, gives notice of a local inquiry which will be held by an inspector on the Minister's behalf. The inquiry is conducted like a court hearing and after hearing both sides and visiting the site, the inspector sends his report with or without recommendations to the minister. At a later date, after consideration of the report, the minister announces his decision.

The main problem with this procedure is that the lay-man who is objecting regards the inquiry as a court hearing. If he puts a good case at the inquiry he expects to win and he will feel that an injustice has been done if he loses. Whereas in reality the purpose of the inquiry is to inform the mind of the minister: it is a fact-finding instrument and the successful presentation of a case is no guide to the result. The minister's decision will be an administrative and not a judicial one: for this reason he may not even follow the recommendations of the inspector's report.

(a) Inquiry rules

Fact-finding as it is, there are however a number of legal rules which an inquiry must observe. It must observe the rules of natural justice which, as has been seen, lay down that both sides must be given reasonable opportunity to state their case and that the inspector holding the inquiry must be free from bias. If Parliament has authorised the making of rules of procedure for the inquiry then these rules must be strictly observed. Similarly any failure by the minister to deal properly with the case, such as a failure to give a reasoned decision, may result in the court intervening to quash the decision. However with these provisos, if Parliament has given the minister a power to make a decision at his own discretion, then the courts cannot interfere with the exercise of that discretion however arbitrary the decision may be. On one reading of the situation local inquiries are not much more than an opportunity for objectors to "blow off steam": on another reading the value of a local inquiry lies in that as a result of it, both sides of the case having been fully stated, a better administrative decision will result.

Most of the examples which follow are of inquiries held where a local authority is in conflict with an individual and the minister has the duty to decide between them. In several such instances Parliament has laid it down that the minister "shall" hold an inquiry, but there are other occasions when the minister from choice decides to hold an inquiry. In other circumstances it may be a public corporation which is the body whose proposals are objected to by individuals, so that the examples, although the most typical, are not intended to be exhaustive.

(b) Town and Country Planning

Parliament has long since laid down that when a person, or a corporation, wishes to develop land, before any development takes place the approval of the local planning authority for the area where the land is situated, must be obtained. This requires that plans must be submitted showing in detail what is involved in the proposed development. If the local planning authority give their approval then the development can take place. If, however, the authority do not approve, or if they approve subject to conditions which the applicant regards as unduly onerous then Parliament has given him the right to appeal to the Minister of Housing and Local Government whose decision is final. In most such appeals the minister will order the holding of a local inquiry. The inquiry will take place in the applicant's locality and will be conducted by an inspector who will report the facts to the minister. The minister will then give his decision. (Town and Country Planning Act 1962.) (See Appendix A).

(c) Housing

When a local authority, charged with the responsibility for improving the housing facilities of its locality, decides that it is necessary to clear an area of unsatisfactory housing it can make what is known as a clearance order. Such an order has to be submitted to the Minister of Housing and Local Government for his confirmation and before giving the order consideration, the minister will require public advertisement to be made of the proposal to submit the order to him. If objections are received to the order then the minister will hold a local inquiry which will be conducted by one of his inspectors. Here again the inspector will report the facts and the minister will ultimately confirm or reject the order. (Housing Act 1957.)

(d) Compulsory Purchase

The wide powers given to local authorities to compel the owners of land to sell it to them for their purposes has become of considerable importance. These powers are very wide indeed and are available for a great many of the purposes of a local authority. The only protection which the individual has is that the local authority must be able to point to an authorising Act of Parliament and that if he objects it is almost certain that the minister of the central government department charged with confirming the particular compulsory purchase order will have to hold a local inquiry into the proposal. The full procedure on the making of a compulsory purchase order will be considered at the end of this chapter.

(e) New Towns

The legislation under which new towns may be designated and then built, requires the holding of a local inquiry if objection is made to the proposed designation. (New Towns Act 1965.)

(f) The Inquiry

The inquiry which is held must fulfil certain fundamental conditions. It is beyond question that the rules of natural justice must be observed and where, by statutory instrument, procedural rules have been enacted these must be strictly observed. Such are the Town and Country Planning (Inquiries Procedure) Rules 1965 and the Compulsory Purchase by Local Authorities (Inquiry Procedure) Rules 1962. These rules aim to provide a court-like basis for the conduct of the inquiry. They deal with such matters as the rights of the parties at the Inquiry, the presentation of the case and the Inspector's duties in holding the inquiry. See Appendix A for the opening page of the 1965 Planning Inquiry Procedure Rules.

Naturally the courts have been confronted with a number of cases arising from these inquiries. In *Nelsovil Ltd.* v. *Minister of Housing and Local Government* (1962) the complainant argued that the minister ought to be bound to follow the findings and recommendations of the inspector. The court firmly rejected this view holding that the decision was entirely for the minister. If however the minister fails to give proper reasons for his decision the court may intervene as it did in *Givaudan & Co., Ltd.* v. *Minister of Housing and Local Government* (1966) when the Minister's decision letter was so confused and obscure that it failed to reveal the Minister's reasons and so was in breach of the Inquiries Procedure Rules and the decision was quashed. See Appendix A, pp. 178, 179, below.

The distinction between an administrative tribunal and a local inquiry is quite fundamental although no attempt has been made to define it by statute. An administrative tribunal is established by an Act of Parliament which lays down its composition and jurisdiction but its outstanding characteristic is that it has all the appearance of a judicial hearing. This appearance is confirmed by the way in which it determines by reasoned judgment all matters coming before it. A local inquiry is also the creature of statute but its task is normally a fact-finding one with little likeness in its conclusion to a judicial determination. As the direct opposite of an administrative tribunal the local inquiry is not concerned with reaching a decision it is, responsible for providing the decision-making person or body with the necessary facts on which a sound decision can be based.

5 THE FRANKS COMMITTEE REPORT AND THE TRIBUNALS AND INQUIRIES ACT 1958

The very nature of administrative law with its ever present problem of law and policy inevitably leads to situations in which decisions are made which do not appear to be just. For example when a ministry inspector has held a public inquiry and then reported to the minister, it must seem to be less than just if the minister then gives a decision contrary to the inspector's recommendation. This is because the party concerned treats the inquiry as if it were a court hearing whereas, as has been seen, it is not a court hearing but a fact-finding body intended to inform the minister. Similarly with delegated legislation it is one thing for a person to find himself baulked in some way by an Act of Parliament but it is quite another for him to find that he is affected by some remote provision of a statutory instrument made by a central government minister. He will treat the former as mistaken but democratic, whereas the latter he will always regard as arbitrary, undemocratic and essentially un-English.

(a) The Donoughmore Report

Because of this conflict much criticism has over the years been directed at both delegated legislation and administrative tribunals and inquiries. It is almost as if the criticism reaches a peak and then has to be allayed by some independent investigation and report. In 1929 Lord HEWART, the then Lord Chief Justice, wrote "*The New Despotism*" attacking the whole system of delegated legislation. An attack by one of such standing caused almost at once the establishment of the Committee on Ministers' Powers which reported in 1932. This report was known as the Donoughmore Report after the chairman. It concluded that delegated legislation was both necessary to modern government and acceptable subject to certain conditions. The Committee produced a number of recommendations which resulted in delegated legislation becoming much more readily accepted as a means of making law of a detailed nature. Criticism of delegated legislation as a system is now uncommon.

(b) Origins of the Franks Report

Following the Second World War and the increasing prominence of the administration under the Labour Government of 1945–1951 much criticism was directed at the development of State intervention in the lives of ordinary people by the administration. This criticism was intensified by the Crichel Down affair of 1954. In this case certain civil servants of the Ministry of Agriculture acted in a very unsatisfactory manner over the tenancy of farm-land which had previously been acquired by compulsory purchase powers. The Minister of Agriculture resigned after an inquiry had found that the department was not without fault in the matter. As a result of this situation the Committee on Administrative Tribunals and Inquiries (Chairman Sir Oliver Franks, now Lord Franks) was appointed to investigate the administrative tribunals and administrative inquiries then existing. The Committee reported in 1957 and as a result of the considerable publicity given to its findings Parliament promptly gave effect to a number of the Report's recommendations in the Tribunal and Inquiries Act 1958. Other minor recommendations were dealt with by instructions from the central Government Minister concerned.

(c) The Report

The Franks Report recognised the value of administrative tribunals pointing out that they were quick to reach a decision, inexpensive to the parties, informal in their conduct of a matter and most were readily accessible all over the country. Whilst there was no argument but that the courts could undertake the work there was much to be said for allowing these tribunals each developing expertise in its own field, to handle the type of matter which had been entrusted to it. They were to be seen as supplementing the court system not as being in conflict with it.

(i) *Essential principles for tribunals and inquiries.*—The Franks Report pinpointed three principles as in their view essential factors in the system of administrative tribunals. It stipulated that such tribunals should be afforded a status of independence comparable to that achieved by the courts, that in arriving at their decisions the tribunals should be as free of departmental influence as possible, and that in the conduct of their affairs they should be governed by the principles of "openness, fairness and impartiality". The previous section on administrative tribunals, through the lengthy comparative table, has already considered the degree of independence bestowed by Parliament on the various tribunals and also has referred to the instances where ministerial influence is prominent. This can occur in the selection of personnel or, in the rare case, where the right of appeal lies to the minister. The attempt to make "openness, fairness and impartiality" characteristics of administrative tribunals continues to be a subject for debate.

Openness, in the sense of public hearings, is a more or less common feature but exceptions are rightly made where individual financial circumstances are under consideration. Fairness is a more difficult matter because where the private interest conflicts with the public interest the result may be anything but "fair" as seen from the standpoint of the loser. Fairness is an ideal. Impartiality is generally the aim of all the tribunals but it is difficult for traffic commissioners and rent tribunals to achieve complete objectivity. Nonetheless efforts are made to give tribunals an appearance of impartiality.

In relation to administrative inquiries the Franks Report, whilst accepting that ministers must retain the right to decide policy matters, nonetheless stressed the view that the inquiries preceding such decisions should also aim to achieve the characteristics of "openness, fairness and impartiality". The rules governing certain of these inquiries, which have already been referred to, do very forcibly create the impression that these principles have been achieved. See Appendix A for a short extract from the 1965 Planning Inquiry Procedure Rules.

(ii) *The Council on Tribunals.*—The Franks Report contained some 95 recommendations most of them concerned with details designed to improve the general standards of administrative tribunals and inquiries. The most important recommendations were given immediate effect by the Tribunals and Inquiries Act 1958 and others were dealt with by ministry circular. Without doubt the most important proposal was for the establishment of a council on tribunals to supervise the work of tribunals and inquiries. This was implemented by the 1958 Act and a council of ten to fifteen members (some having responsibility for Scotland) has been established which is appointed by and is answerable to the Lord Chancellor. The duties of the council are to keep under review the constitution and working of the tribunals listed in the Act, and also those tribunals which have been so designated since the Act. As well as making an annual report to Parliament, the council can deal with particular matters concerning tribunals either at the request of the Lord Chancellor or of its own volition. The Lord Chancellor or any minister must consult the council before making procedural rules affecting a tribunal or inquiry. There were, of course, certain teething troubles with the council but these are gradually being put right: for one thing it was found that by an oversight members of the council were not entitled to attend certain tribunals at work: another snag was that certain tribunals lay outside the supervision of the council: again although the council had to be consulted before procedural rules for a tribunal were issued, new tribunals could be set up by Parliament without any consultation with the council: in connection with inquiries the council was limited to those the minister was compelled to hold and they could not deal with those which he had a discretion to hold. Gradually these matters are being remedied: the latest measure is the Tribunals and Inquiries Act 1966 which extends the council's supervision to certain previously excepted inquiries and generally continues the tidying up process.

(iii) *Work of the council.*—The value of the council is considerable and not least on the occasions when it has produced special reports drawing attention to weakness in matters affecting administrative tribunals and inquiries. In "The Chalkpit Case", *Buxton* v. *Minister of Housing and Local Government* (1961), the Council drew attention to a very undesirable factor in a town and country planning inquiry case, where the minister having held a local inquiry and received his inspector's report then consulted behind the scenes with another ministry. In the result the minister decided the case against the advice of his inspector and presumably influenced by the information from this other ministry which had not been disclosed to the parties attending the inquiry. The council drew attention to the fact that such action inevitably appeared to be unjust. In the result the Town and Country Planning Appeals (Inquiries Procedure) Rules 1962 (re-issued in 1965) were produced; one rule of which means that in future any such information obtained from another ministry by the minister would have to be disclosed and also be the subject of cross-examination.

A second example was the report submitted on the *Packington Estate, Islington,* case in February 1966. The crux of the complaint in this planning case was that after a local inquiry into a local authority scheme for redevelopment the minister refused planning permission, but then without informing the objectors he approved a modified scheme after secret discussions with the local authority. The council drew attention to the inevitable criticism on the part of the objectors, pointing out that, whilst such third parties to a planning application have no legal rights at all under the existing planning legislation, in this instance the Minister's conduct could be criticised on two grounds. First the decision letter refusing permission was misleading in the light of what followed, and then the failure to afford the objectors an opportunity to see and comment on the revised plan was bound to appear unjust. Although no obvious change resulted from this report the matter had a thorough airing in Parliament and it seems a reasonable hope that a repetition of the incident is unlikely.

(iv) *Further improvements.*—Other improvements recommended by the Franks Report and given effect by the 1958 Act include:

(i)   appointments of lawyer-chairmen to be from a panel of names to be maintained by the Lord Chancellor—Section 3

(ii)   dismissal of members of administrative tribunals to be subject to the Lord Chancellor's consent—Section 5

(iii) the Council on Tribunals to make general recommendations for appointment of members of administrative tribunals —Section 4

(iv) right of appeal on a point of law to the High Court—Section 9

(v)   Tribunals and Ministers to give reasons for their decisions when demanded—Section 12

(vi) no exclusion of judicial control to be permissible—Section 11

Improvements brought about informally were that proceedings should be held in public save in exceptional circumstances, and that parties should be legally represented if they wished.

Naturally not all the recommendations of the committee were accepted and implemented. The provisions for an appeal on the merits of the case fall short, in a number of instances, of the recommendation that there should be a right of appeal on fact, law and merits to an appeal tribunal, save where the lower tribunal is exceptionally strong. In particular there is no appeal from a rent tribunal except on a point of law and yet in 1965 these tribunals heard over 6,000 cases. And there are still a few instances, in contravention of the report's proposals, where an appeal from a tribunal lies to the Minister. Again the Act does not give effect to all the committee's recommendations about the appointment of chairmen and members of tribunals, nor the recommendation that the inspectorate for administrative inquiries should come under the Lord Chancellor and so be separated from the ministerial department responsible for deciding the matter. A further recommendation which was not implemented was that before an administrative inquiry was held the minister concerned should provide a statement of the ministerial policy relevant to the particular case. It should, of course, be said that the Government's refusal to implement these various recommendations was not an arbitrary decision, reasons having been given in each case.

6 COMPULSORY PURCHASE PROCEDURE BY LOCAL AUTHORITIES

The conflict between individual freedom and public body control has become increasingly acute, and the harsh feeling engendered is nowhere more apparent than in the exercise of compulsory purchase powers by a local authority. Such powers have been available to local authorities for many years but it is only since the end of the war in 1945 that they have come to be used on a vast scale.

Today these powers are available to cover the acquisition of land required for any of the following services: aerodromes, allotments, caravan sites, children services, civil defence, civic restaurants, coast protection, education, fire, health, highways, housing, libraries, markets, offices, parks and open spaces, planning, police, smallholdings, town development, water and welfare. And this list is not exhaustive. Different conditions depending upon the Act of Parliament concerned, have to be fulfilled by the various kinds of local authority, but the present tendency is to give ever greater powers as time passes; for example, the Greater London Council set up by the London Government Act 1963 was given power by that Act to compulsorily purchase land for any of its functions.

The justification for allowing these powers to local authorities is the modern demand that the public interest should take precedence over private convenience. Hence any decision by a local authority that it must have land for a specific purpose, leading to a refusal by the owner to sell voluntarily, may very well result in a short time in the land becoming the subject of compulsory purchase procedure. As might be expected so gross an interference with personal liberty is hedged about with certain restrictions and it is thus necessary that a study of the procedure should follow.

(a) Requirements

The over-riding factors are that the local authority must in all cases first be able to point to an Act of Parliament permitting, directly or by inference, such compulsory action; and then show that the authorisation of the Minister named as the confirming body in the Act of Parliament has been obtained, and the various other statutory requirements with regard to notice and publicity fulfilled. No compulsory purchase order can ever be made without these matters being shown. It is thus clear that the compulsory purchase order process is in its essence a form of delegated legislation.

The procedure is laid down in the Acquisition of Land (Authorisation Procedure) Act 1946, Section 1 and Schedule 1 Part 1 and in the Compulsory Purchase of Land Regulations 1949 (S.I. 1949 No. 507). The 1946 Act extends to all statutorily bestowed compulsory purchase powers whether granted by legislation before 1946 or incorporated by direct reference, as is now customary, in legislation passed since 1946. There is thus a uniform procedural code for all such purchases with the one exception of the land acquired by compulsion under Part 3 of the Housing Act 1957 where the procedure is separately enacted but is basically similar.

(b) Preparing for the order

The first step is for the members of the local authority to decide the exact area of land which it needs to acquire. The officers of the local authority then prepare a plan which shows exactly the area involved, and the local authority then makes a compulsory purchase order relating to this land. The order must be in the form prescribed by the regulations and must specify the statutory powers which the local authority deems itself entitled to use. The local authority must then follow strictly the requirements of the regulations, which involves advertising the making of the order and the intention to submit it for confirmation. This advertisement must appear in a local newspaper or newspapers for two successive weeks. It must be in a prescribed form which involves setting out fully the contents of the order and it must indicate the period within which objections may be made. This period is stipulated to be not less than twenty-one days. At the same time the local authority must serve every owner or tenant of any part of the land affected, with a copy of the published notice. If appropriate such notice may be affixed to the property instead of being served personally, but here the Minister must give his approval to the arrangement.

If no objections are entered or maintained the Minister can confirm the order forthwith as submitted or as modified by him. In the much more likely instance of objections being entered to the proposal, then the minister must hold a local public inquiry at which the objectors and the local authority can state their respective cases.

(c) Report received by Minister

The inquiry has to be held in accordance with the Compulsory Purchase by Local Authorities (Inquiry Procedure) Rules 1962. When the inquiry is complete the minister receives the report of his inspector and in his administrative capacity the Minister will decide whether to confirm or reject the order as drawn, or to confirm it modified in some respect. In coming to his decision he is not bound by his inspector's recommendations and he is not limited to considering only evidence given at the inquiry.

If the Minister decides to confirm the order as drawn or as amended, notice of the decision must be advertised in a local newspaper or newspapers and also given to all the individuals whose property is affected by the order and who originally received notice of the order.

(d) The order

The order takes effect from the date of the first publication of the minister's decision. It can only be challenged in the courts within six weeks of the operative date and then only on one of two grounds. Either that the order is in some way *"ultra vires"* the local authority making it or the Minister confirming it, or that there has been a failure to comply with the procedural requirements of the 1946 Act and/or the rules or regulations. And even on these grounds the court may overlook a technical fault if the interests of the complainant have not been substantially affected.

Once the order has been confirmed and published the local authority may serve a notice to treat on the owners of the land concerned. This leads to negotiations, usually by professional valuers, about the compensation to be paid. If agreement is reached the purchase is completed by conveyance like a normal sale of land. If no agreement is reached about the compensation to be paid, the Lands Tribunal can be given the task of settling the value of the land. If no owner can be traced, the estimated value is paid into court to await his appearance. If an owner completely refuses to co-operate, the acquiring authority can pay the compensation into court, execute a deed vesting the property in itself and, if absolutely necessary, obtain the court's assistance to have the former owner turned off the land.

(e) Special procedures

Where a local authority desires to acquire, compulsorily, land in any of the following categories then special procedures as set out in Schedule 1 Part 3 of the 1946 Act are required to be observed.

    (i)   Land belonging to another local authority;

    (ii) Land belonging to a statutory undertaker *e.g.* Post Office, Gas Board;

    (iii) Land belonging to the National Trust;

    (iv) Land forming part of a common or open space; and

    (v)   Land on which an ancient monument stands or which is of archaeological interest.

Such compulsory purchase orders are normally required to undergo special Parliamentary procedure before becoming effective, but where a minister is prepared to certify the reasonableness of the proposal the need for Parliamentary approval can be avoided.

(f) Court decisions

As might be expected arguments over compulsory purchase orders frequently reach the courts. In *Brown* v. *Minister of Housing and Local Government* (1953) it came to light, after the inquiry had been held and the order confirmed, that one person affected had not been served with the appropriate notices or given the opportunity to object. The court without hesitation quashed the order so far as it affected the premises occupied by that person.

In *Hazeldine* v. *Minister of Housing and Local Government* (1959) the point at issue was the fundamental one of whether or not the statute relied on permitted the making of a compulsory purchase order for the particular purpose intended. The question was whether or not the purchase of land for "the functions" of a police authority included the right to compulsorily purchase land in order to build police houses. The court decided that it did.

In *Smith* v. *East Elloe Rural District Council* (1956) the point taken was whether the six weeks' time limit for challenging a compulsory purchase order applied if the order was, as alleged, made and confirmed in bad faith. The House of Lords decided that the six weeks period for challenging the order was absolute. An alternative remedy in damages against the individuals concerned might lie, but the order would have to stand.

The latest case in this field is *Webb* v. *Minister of Housing and Local Government* (1965) in which a compulsory purchase order made by the Bognor Regis Council and confirmed by the Minister was successfully challenged.   The objector contended, amongst other things, that the order was *"ultra vires"* the council and the Minister since it was made for coast protection purposes but it took more land than was necessary for the coast protection work, because the council intended to provide a promenade as a result of the works. The Court of Appeal accepted this argument and declared that the compulsory purchase order was invalid.   This case is a good illustration of the very strict approach of the courts to the legal issues involved in the making of a compulsory purchase order.

Chapter 5

The Protection of the Individual by the Judiciary

1 INTRODUCTION

In the preceding chapters the main concern has been to study the way in which law is made. It has been seen how the law-making activities of Parliament, the courts and the administration together result in a tremendous bulk of new law. As a direct result there are inevitable conflicts with individual members of the public and the judiciary is then called upon to examine the powers in question and possibly prevent the body concerned from carrying out its intentions. In this chapter the first objective will be to discover the *grounds* on which the courts have in the past been prepared to intervene and assist the individual. These grounds can be grouped under the headings, infringements of the rules of natural justice, excess of power (the *"ultra vires"* doctrine), and what are called errors of law appearing on the face of the record. Each of these will be examined in turn. Then the second part of the chapter will consider the actual *remedies* used by the courts to force the person or organisation concerned to act in accordance with the law.

In a sense this chapter is the balance to what has gone before. In chapters 2, 3 and 4 the powers of the law-making bodies were explained, now it is necessary to consider what kind of restriction the judiciary is able to impose on those bodies and under what circumstances. It must be considered basic to this point that in certain instances the judiciary is absolutely powerless. If Parliament, as the supreme power in the State, passes a law which is oppressive the courts cannot refuse to enforce that law. Again if Parliament gives a minister power to act in a particular matter and stipulates in specific terms at the same time that the courts shall not review his decision, then the minister is outside the court's control. Although this is so, it is, of course, not likely that Parliament will enact oppressive legislation or that it will, save in the direst emergency, give such powers to a minister. But if this happens the remedy lies with other bodies than the judiciary. Public opinion and the press continue to play a vital part in the protection of the individual from unjust laws and improper administrative interference, but these and all other such methods of imposing checks on the law-makers are outside the immediate scope of this chapter.

2 THE GROUNDS FOR INTERVENTION

(a) The Rules of Natural Justice

The courts insist as a fundamental obligation that any person or body, which is exercising a judicial function, must comply with the rules of natural justice. The basis of this view is that it is implicit in the power to act as a judge that these rules will be observed. If the power to act as a judge has been bestowed by Parliament then the courts regard the inclusion of the observance of these rules as implied in the appointment. It is assumed that Parliament would never intend any person or organisation, placed in such a position, to flout these rules.

The expression "The rules of natural justice" involves two separate characteristics: (i) "*Nemo judex in causa sua potest*", "no one can be judge in his own cause" and (ii) "*Audi alteram partem*", "hear both sides of the case". Each of these headings will be considered in turn.

(i) "*No one can be judge in his own cause*".—This has been taken to mean that anyone who has a possible bias in a matter should not act as a judge in it. In *Dimes* v. *Grand Junction Canal Co.* (1852) an order made by the Lord Chancellor was quashed when it later came to light that at the time when he gave his decision he held a number of shares in the company concerned. This was not because there was any suggestion that the Lord Chancellor had actually shown bias in the case but because "justice should not only be done but should manifestly and undoubtedly be seen to be done" (Lord HEWART, C.J.). On the same basis a decision by a magistrate in matrimonial proceedings was quashed when it appeared that the magistrate was a close friend of the mother of one of the parties. *Cottle* v. *Cottle* (1939). It will be noticed that it is not solely a question of financial advantage or, as the technical phrase has it, "pecuniary interest"; the rule is infringed whenever there is a real likelihood of bias. In *Cooper* v. *Wilson* (1937) a chief constable who had dismissed a police constable sat in with the body which was hearing the constable's appeal against the dismissal. The body's confirmation of the chief constable's decision was quashed as being in breach of this rule.

These three cases are all examples of occasions when the courts accepted that the decision of the body concerned could not be allowed to stand because of the bias apparent in the adjudication. Sometimes, in contrast, however, even more apparent instances of bias in a "judge" are allowed to stand. In *Franklin* v. *Minister of Town and Country Planning* (1947) the case arose over the designation of the new town to be built at Stevenage, Hertfordshire. The minister, who was given by statute the responsibility for designating sites for new towns after the holding of public inquiries, went to a meeting at Stevenage about the proposed designation, before any public inquiry was held, and said "It is going to be done". His later designation of the site was challenged on the grounds of bias but the House of Lords refused to intervene, finding that the minister's decision was administrative, a policy decision, and not judicial. Provided the minister observed the procedure stipulated in the statute, the decision was entirely a matter for himself. Ministerial bias then, in this situation, was not a ground for challenge. However by way of contrast in *Errington* v. *Minister of Health* (1935) a decision on slum clearance by the minister was quashed when he had obtained information, and had had inspections made, behind the backs of the objectors. The court held that in hearing objections the minister's role was judicial, even though his ultimate decision was administrative, and so in dealing with the objections, the rules of natural justice needed to be observed.

This distinction between a judicial and an administrative decision is a major difficulty in administrative law. If a decision is judicial the court can intervene, if it is administrative the court cannot. But the drawing of the dividing line as seen in the two following cases is a constant matter for argument. A trade union member, who was expelled by his Union without being given notice of the charge on which he was expelled, obtained a declaration that such expulsion was void. The union's decision was a judicial decision and was taken in breach of the rules of natural justice. (*Annamunthodo* v. *Oilfield Workers' Trade Union* (1961).) A member of the Jockey Club had his trainer's licence withdrawn by the stewards without, as he alleged, being given full notice of the charge or the opportunity to call all his witnesses at the hearing. The court held that this was an administrative matter for the Club and the complainant was, strictly, not even entitled to a hearing. The rules of natural justice were not relevant. (*Russell* v. *Duke of Norfolk* (1949).) This difficult distinction will be met again: particularly in the discussion of the remedy of the order of *certiorari*.

(ii) *"Hear both sides of the case".*—This rule, at its simplest, means that both parties must be given an opportunity to present their case in full.

Inevitably this includes knowing the charges which are the basis of the case and of having an adequate opportunity to prepare a case to answer the charges. In *Annamunthodo* v. *Oilfield Workers' Trade Union* (1961), referred to above, the expulsion of a trade union member was held to be invalid because the member was neither given notice of the particular charge on which he was expelled nor given an opportunity to answer it. The same reasoning led the House of Lords in *Ridge* v. *Baldwin* (1964) to declare invalid the purported dismissal of their chief constable by the Brighton Watch Committee, where the committee had failed to give Ridge the opportunity to appear before them to answer charges of negligence and unfitness to hold the office of chief constable. Again there had been a failure to observe the rules of natural justice. By way of contrast, however, the Privy Council, in *Vidyodaya University of Ceylon* v. *Silva* (1964), refused to assist a professor who had been dismissed by the university. The dismissal of a servant by a master under an ordinary contract of employment is not a situation in which the courts will intervene. On the other hand the Privy Council, in another recent case from Ceylon, *Maradana Mosque (Board of Trustees)* v. *Badi-ud-Din-Mahmud* (1966), quashed the decision of the Minister of Education there, where the complainant body had not been given an opportunity to answer one of two charges made against it. From the cases quoted, the difficulty, of perceiving whether or not the court will hold that the decision is sufficiently of a judicial nature to warrant the application of the rules of natural justice, is apparent.

The argument may turn not only on the awareness of the charges to be answered but also on the conduct of the "trial". In *Local Government Board* v. *Arlidge* (1915) the House of Lords very firmly denied the right of an individual to require court-like treatment at a statutory inquiry. There the complainant sought to compel the board to hear him in person before confirming a closing order on a house and also to insist on their allowing him to see the official report of the inspector at the inquiry. On neither ground would the court assist him. Since 1915 the position has been much changed by later legislation so that it is as well to have this in mind when dealing with the *Arlidge* case. Nonetheless it remains effective on its facts.

Sometimes the argument will turn on the admission of or failure to admit certain matters: in *R.* v. *Deputy Industrial Injuries Commissioner,*

Ex parte Jones (1962) the Commissioner, after an oral hearing, obtained specialist information behind the scenes which affected his decision. The decision was quashed because, the court decided, the parties ought to have been given notice of this information and given opportunity to question it if they thought fit. A similar conclusion was reached in *Errington* v. *Minister of Health* (1935), explained above. A more recent instance having the same result was *R.* v. *Paddington Rent Tribunal, Ex parte Bell Properties, Ltd.* (1949) where the decision of the Tribunal was quashed because it had taken into account a factor about the height of ceilings without giving the owning company the opportunity to answer it.

Throughout, the problem is to ascertain when the courts will be prepared to intervene; the basis on which they will intervene is apparent from the cases. It must not be overlooked, however, that in this field as well as in others the supremacy of Parliament is a factor. If Parliament expressly or by implication indicates that a decision is to be made by a particular person or body, irrespective of consideration of the rules of natural justice, then in such a situation the courts are not able to question that decision. In *Wilkinson* v. *Barking Corporation* (1948) by statute a decision about superannuation fell to be dealt with by a local authority and, on appeal, by the Minister of Housing and Local Government. Both the local authority and the minister had a pecuniary interest in the result of the case since it was from their funds that the claim would be met, but the courts would not assist an applicant, who alleged bias because, they said, Parliament had given the authority to the minister even though it must have foreseen that his decision would be in breach of the rules of natural justice.

(b) The doctrine of Ultra Vires

The Latin words *"ultra vires"* mean "beyond the powers"; and the doctrine of *ultra vires* means that bodies which are created by Parliament can only lawfully do those things for which Parliament has given them powers. If they exceed the powers given to them the acts done are said to be *"ultra vires"*.

The doctrine has particular significance in public law since so many of the bodies with which public law is concerned have been created by Act of Parliament: for example, local authorities (except certain ancient corporations created by Royal Charter), administrative tribunals, administrative inquiries and public corporations. It is thus always possible for the courts to examine the activities of these bodies and, if so found, to declare those activities to be *"ultra vires"*.

(i) *Legal power of council.*—Perhaps the simplest example of this sort of intervention is where a local authority plans to do something and then a ratepayer objects that they have no legal power to carry out their intention. In the *Attorney-General* v. *Fulham Corporation* (1921) the corporation wished to provide a municipal laundry service: when challenged, the only authorising power to which they could point was one enabling them to provide washhouses at which ratepayers could wash their own clothes. Thus the intended provision of the laundry was held to be *"ultra vires"*. The difficulty with this doctrine from the local authority point of view is that if it has spent money on some service which is held to be *"ultra vires"*, it is possible that the government's district auditor, who annually checks the accounts of local authorities, may require those members who authorised the expenditure to reimburse the rate fund. He is said to "surcharge" the councillors responsible. In practice this rarely happens save where councillors have defied advice given to them. The recent Maud Committee Report (1967) has recommended the abolition of the district auditor's power to surcharge.

A special difficulty with local authorities, which cannot be completely ignored, is that whilst county councils, urban and rural district councils are the creation of statute, the boroughs have to be divided into two categories—those created by Royal Charter under statutory provision since the Municipal Corporations Act 1835 and those ancient boroughs which have Royal Charters from before this date. This latter class of authority can claim that under their Charter they are free from any statutory restriction and so are not subject at all to the *"ultra vires"* doctrine and, consequently, any possibility of surcharge. A case decided at first instance in 1943, the *Attorney-General* v. *Leicester Corporation*, lends support to this view. In it Leicester Corporation was held entitled to purchase a bus service which was actually operating outside its boundaries. Such a purchase would have been *"ultra vires"* any other type of local authority. There is much academic argument about the position; it is sufficient for the purposes of this book that the student should know that in connection with the *"ultra vires"* doctrine such a distinction between the various classes of local authority is made.

(ii) *Exercising discretion unreasonably.*—Other examples of cases in which actions of local authorities have been challenged on the basis of the *"ultra vires"* rule are:

(1) *Attorney-General* v. *Crayford Urban District Council* (1962), where it was decided that a local authority, exercising its powers of general

management in the provision of council housing, could properly arrange insurance of the contents of such property for its tenants and include the premium in the rent, i.e. it was not *"ultra vires"* for a housing authority to include insurance premiums in the rent of a council house.

(2) *Prescott* v. *Birmingham Corporation* (1954) where the corporation's plan to provide cheap fares for the elderly using the municipal bus service was held to be *"ultra vires"*. Legislation later extended the powers of local authorities to provide these facilities.

(3) *Roberts* v. *Hopwood* (1925) where the Poplar Borough Council aiming to be model employers paid a minimum rate of wages which was above the local prevailing rate. The district auditor surcharged the council £5,000 which he estimated to be the amount which the council had paid (or, as the House of Lords put it, "given away") more than it need have done. There was, as might be guessed, a political background to this situation and it became something of a *"cause celebre"*.

(4) *Taylor* v. *Munrow* (1960) where the St. Pancras Borough Council decided for political reasons not to increase the rents of certain of their tenants who were in requisitioned property. This was contrary to the advice given to them by the government of the day which had just had passed the Rent Act 1957 making for general increases in rent. In the result the district auditor surcharged the councillors responsible for the loss of revenue to the rate fund.

In the last two cases it will be noted that the *"ultra vires"* rule was applied because the council acted unreasonably. In the first case the council were able to pay such wages as they thought fit: in the second case the rent to be charged was in a general sense in their discretion: yet in both cases the exercise of the council's discretion in an unreasonable way made the decisions *"ultra vires"*.

This doctrine of *"ultra vires"* has been applied to other administrative bodies: in *R.* v. *Blackpool Rent Tribunal, Ex parte Ashton* (1948), a tribunal decision was quashed as being *"ultra vires"* when the tribunal had accepted as "furnished" a tenancy which on examination a court held not to be furnished. As the tribunal could only hear cases where there was "a furnished tenancy" it is not difficult to see the logic of the court's decision.

Again, in *White and Collins* v. *Minister of Health* (1939), the Minister confirmed a compulsory purchase order to take land for housing purposes. There was an exemption in the Act of Parliament for land which formed part of "a park". The court decided that part of this land was "a park": the minister's confirmation was thus ineffective for the order was *"ultra vires"*.

A further example involving another central Government Minister was in *R.* v. *Minister of Transport, Ex parte Upminster Services, Ltd.* (1934) where a licence condition imposed by the Minister was held to be unreasonable and hence *"ultra vires"*.

A text-book distinction is frequently drawn between what is called "substantive *ultra vires*" on the one hand and "procedural *ultra vires*" on the other. By "substantive *ultra vires*" is meant that the act complained of is outside the powers of the statutory body concerned. The case of *White and Collins* v. *Minister of Health* (1939) referred to above is just one instance of "substantive *ultra vires*": another would be *Prescott* v. *Birmingham Corporation* (1954), also referred to above, where the corporation at that time lacked the necessary legal power to implement the scheme which they wished to introduce. By "procedural *ultra vires*" is meant that the body concerned has in some way failed to comply with the procedural obligations which the authorising Act of Parliament had attached to the powers in question. For example, a failure to consult the bodies which Parliament stipulated should be consulted, or a failure to publish as required, would fall within the term "procedural *ultra vires*".

(iii) *Delegation of power.*—It will readily be appreciated that the term *"ultra vires"* can be extended very widely. In addition to the situations covered by the preceding cases there are a number of other situations in which the term *"ultra vires"* can be properly used. Where the power to act has been given to one body, if action is taken by some other person or body, then the courts will almost certainly regard the decision as *"ultra vires"*. The case of *Allingham* v. *Minister of Agriculture and Fisheries* (1948), decided that a power delegated by the minister to a local agricultural executive committee could not then be delegated to an officer. This exemplifies the maxim *"delegatus non potest delegare"*—"a delegate is not able to delegate". The same finding of *"ultra vires"* would apply if the body authorised was not properly constituted or if the appropriate procedure laid down had not been followed.

(iv) *Improper use of a power.*—On similar reasoning a power which has been given to a body by Parliament which is used for some improper purpose by that body is *"ultra vires"*. In *Sydney Municipal Council* v. *Campbell* (1925), the council misused a power to compulsorily purchase land; the council purported to purchase the land for the purpose of making streets, whereas in fact it was acquiring the land because its value was likely to increase rapidly and the council wanted to benefit from this. This misuse of the power meant that any compulsory purchase order would be *"ultra vires"*. A recent example of the same sort occurred in *Webb* v. *Minister of Housing and Local Government* (1965) where the Bognor Regis council made a compulsory purchase order to acquire land for coast protection work. The minister confirmed this order. It then transpired that the council had included in the order more land than was strictly necessary for the coast protection work intending to provide also a public promenade. The compulsory purchase order was declared invalid on the grounds of *"ultra vires"*.

(v) *Irrelevant matters considered.*—A further basis on which a decision of a public body can be declared *"ultra vires"* is where it takes into account factors which are strictly not relevant to the matter under consideration. *Roberts* v. *Hopwood* (1925) which has been outlined above was decided on the basis that the council had taken certain irrelevant matters into consideration and that this had caused their discretion to be exercised in an unreasonable way. Frequent examples of this kind of *"ultra vires"* decision are provided by local authorities, who, in town and country planning applications, attach conditions to an approval which are held to be irrelevant. A clear example is *Hall & Co., Ltd.* v. *Shoreham-by-Sea Urban District Council* (1964) where the council in granting a planning permission attached a condition which would have caused the company to construct a road on their own land and virtually dedicate it to the public without compensation. This was held to be unreasonable and *"ultra vires"*. The conditions which a council can attach to a planning permission "must fairly and reasonably relate to the permitted development. The planning authority are not at liberty to use their powers for an ulterior object however desirable that object may seem to them to be in the public interest" (Lord DENNING, M.R.).

From what has been said above it will now be apparent that the doctrine of *"ultra vires"* has been applied to many different situations and is very much more complex than the apparently straightforward meaning from which this discussion started, of some action being "beyond the powers" contained in certain statutory provisions.

(c) Error of Law on the face of the Record

A much less important ground for intervention is where the decision of an inferior tribunal reveals on its face an error of law.

In every such case the supervisory power of the High Court through its divisional court enables the decision to be quashed by an order of *certiorari*.

This particular method of control, having largely fallen into disuse, was given new life in 1952 in the case *R.* v. *Northumberland Compensation Appeal Tribunal, Ex parte Shaw.* There the court quashed the decision of the tribunal because its determination revealed a mistaken interpretation of the law; the tribunal had failed in assessing compensation to take into account the applicant's previous service with a local authority. The court held that the tribunal should have done so. The tribunal's actual award therefore revealed an error of law on the face of the record. The various documents which can make up the "record" are an added complication since the courts have not yet settled the matter; in general it is likely to be held that the "record" includes the pleadings, the formal decision order and any documents on which the decision is based. The Tribunals and Inquiries Act 1958 has added to this ground for review by enacting, in section 12, that reasons must be given for decisions and clearly this means that, whether written or oral, these reasons are to be incorporated in the record; the result being that this ground for review is much more likely to be involved than formerly.

A 1960 case, *R.* v. *Minister of Housing and Local Government, Ex parte Chichester R.D.C.*, is a good example. There the minister confirmed a "purchase notice" served on the local authority on grounds which were held to be improper. The Act of Parliament required the minister to confirm if satisfied that the land in question had become "incapable of reasonably beneficial use in its existing state". In his decision the minister purported to confirm on the ground that the land was "substantially less useful". This confirmation was quashed because of the error of law appearing on the face of the record. Another example is afforded by the case illustrated on pp. 178, 179, below.

(d) Exclusion of Judicial Review by Act of Parliament.

Having now explained the grounds on which the courts can intervene in the decisions of administrative bodies it is perhaps an appropriate point at which to emphasise that it is not every decision which can be called in question. As has been seen in the discussion of the rules of natural justice it is quite possible for Parliament to delegate a power to a minister or other public body or officer and in doing so to exclude review by the courts. This is but one facet of the doctrine of the sovereignty or supremacy of Parliament. But the courts will only recognise this exclusion where they are satisfied by the specific words of the Act that this was the intention of Parliament. Where they do so find then the decision is beyond challenge. On the other hand just because the Act says that a decision is to be "final" this does not mean that the courts cannot intervene. The word "final" in this context is taken to mean "final on the facts" and not "final on the law", thus leaving the way open for judicial review.

3   THE REMEDIES

Once the courts are persuaded that there are grounds for their intervention in an actual matter where an administrative body has reached a particular decision, then the question immediately arises as to what remedy should be made available. This section of the chapter will be concerned with these remedies.

First of all there are the prerogative orders which the Queen's Bench Divisional Court can issue; these are *mandamus,* prohibition and *certiorari.* As the word "prerogative" implies, these orders were originally issued by the Monarch, in the form of writs, to keep in check the lesser courts which at one time flourished throughout the realm. These writs have been re-named as orders but they retain, as will be seen, traces of their origin in various ways, not least in that they cannot lie against the Monarch. Each of the three orders will be examined in turn and examples will be given of instances where applications for the order have, and have not, been successful.

The remainder of the section will be given up to the other remedies which the courts may use where the orders are not appropriate. The equitable remedies of the declaratory judgment and an injunction are of especial significance since, in particular, the former is very frequently sought. Public bodies can be relied upon to observe a statement by declaration as to the legal rights of the parties, and proceedings for a declaration are more straightforward than those leading to the issue of one of the prerogative orders. The remedy is thus much favoured. The obtaining of the prerogative writ of *habeas corpus* will fall for consideration at this point although, concerned as it is with improper detention, its real relevance will be more apparent in chapter 6 which is concerned with the liberties of the subject. There then remains the possible remedy of an action for damages either alone or linked with some other remedy, but this, being the standard form of remedy in most civil actions, seems somewhat mundane by comparison with the more colourful remedies which precede it.

These are all the judicial remedies and between them they provide a comprehensive panacea for the ills of administrative bodies. It is felt, however, that a concluding note to the chapter ought to ensure that no-one loses sight of the other non-judicial methods by other bodies which are designed to achieve the same end. Many of these other methods will have been met previously but it is important that their existence should not be overlooked, since it is not by the courts alone that the individual citizen is protected.

(a) The Prerogative Orders

(i) *Mandamus.*—This prerogative order is issued by the Queen's Bench Divisional court and is used to ensure that public bodies carry out the duties imposed upon them by law. The word "*Mandamus*" means "we order" and once the court issues the order a failure to comply is a contempt of court. It is not unknown for such a contempt by a public body to result in the individual members being sent to prison. In 1922 in *R. v. Poplar Borough Council*, a *Mandamus* was issued ordering the Poplar Borough Council to collect in a rate for the purposes of the London County Council as it was required to do by Act of Parliament. When the members of the Poplar Council deliberately failed to carry out the court's order they were arrested and put in prison for contempt. Such a drastic step is very rare, however, because normally a public body will immediately obey a court order.

The thinking which underlies the order of *mandamus* is that right through legal history the courts have always been prepared to provide a remedy where they are satisfied that there has been an obvious failure to obtain justice. Thus if a public body is charged with a responsibility by Act of Parliament and that public body fails or refuses to carry out its task then in those circumstances the appropriate remedy is for the divisional court to order the public body to do its duty. This is done by the issue of an order of *mandamus*.

A *mandamus* will only issue where the public body is under a duty to act: it will not issue to force such a body to exercise a discretion in a particular way. The court takes the view that where Parliament has given a public body a discretion, only that body can exercise that discretion. So although the court will order the public body to exercise its discretion one way or the other where it has failed to, it will never substitute its own decision for that of the public body.

Again where the public body carries out its duty but does so in an unsatisfactory way as, for example, where it has failed to give the parties a proper hearing or failed to give reasons for its decision, then the court may issue *mandamus*. Instances of where *mandamus* has been granted are:

(1) directed to a rent tribunal which had refused to deal with an application to it because it wrongly thought that it had no power to take the case.

> *R. v. Paddington South Rent Tribunal* (1955)

(2) directed to a local authority which had refused to register a change of ownership in respect of a hackney carriage licence (a taxi licence) because it had misunderstood the basis of registration.

> *R. v. Weymouth Corporation, Ex parte Teletax (Weymouth) Ltd.* (1947)

(3) directed to the Registrar of Joint Stock Companies to register a company

> *R. v. Registrar of Joint Stock Companies, Ex parte More* (1931)

(4) directed to an administrative tribunal where it had failed to hold a proper hearing before coming to its decision.

> *R. v. Housing Appeal Tribunal* (1920)

(5) directed to a local authority requiring it to produce its accounts for the examination of a ratepayer as required by law.

> *R. v. Bedwellty Urban District Council, Ex parte Price* (1934)

(6) directed to a central Government body which failed to answer a question which by statute it was required to answer.

> *Board of Education v. Rice* (1911)

(7) directed to a public body or public officer which/who failed to give, as required by law, adequate reasons for its/his decision.

> *Re Poyser and Mills Arbitration* (1964) (an arbitrator's award set aside)

The order of *mandamus* lies within the discretion of the court and there are, derived from the previous cases, a number of rules which can be stated as principles affecting the order. Before an application can succeed it must be shown that the public body or officer concerned has been asked to carry out the duty in question and has refused or failed to do so. Further that the application is being made within a reasonable time of the refusal or failure to act and that the applicant has a sufficiently personal interest in the matter to found his claim for the issue of the order. *Mandamus* will not be granted if some other remedy is laid down in the statute placing the obligation on the public body. In *Pasmore* v. *Oswaldtwistle Urban District Council* (1898) the Council were by Act of Parliament responsible for providing sewers to drain their district. The applicant was the owner of a paper mill who claimed that the council had failed to provide adequate drainage for his premises, and because of this he sought a *mandamus*. The Act of Parliament in question, however, contained a provision under which complaints were to be made to the local government board: if the board failed to persuade the council to carry out its duty it was open to the board to apply for an order of *mandamus*. In these circumstances the court held that *mandamus* would not be issued at the behest of a private individual but only on an application from the board. This kind of statutory provision is not uncommon. Another example is that if a local education authority fails to provide proper educational facilities as it is required to do by the Education Act 1944 the Minister of Education may give the authority instructions which he may enforce by an application for *mandamus*. In the result it seems unlikely that a private individual will be able to obtain a *mandamus* directed to a local education authority. In the case of some statutes imposing very general duties on a public body such as to provide an efficient supply of gas or electricity it is almost certain that the courts will not attempt to enforce such duties by *mandamus*. In at least one case they have been ordered by Act of Parliament not to do so (Transport Act 1962 section 3). If on the other hand the duty in question is held not to be a public duty at all but a domestic or internal matter, as in *R.* v. *Dunsheath ex parte Meredith* (1951) where the duty in question was laid down in a University's statutes, then the court will not issue *mandamus*. A recent case decided on the same basis was *Thorne* v. *University of London* (1966) where the applicant wanted the court to order the investigation of his examination results. He was not successful.

As a prerogative order *mandamus* will not be issued against the Crown nor generally against Crown servants except where a duty is owed to a member of the public. It has on occasions been issued against central government departments and more frequently, as has been seen, against local authorities, administrative tribunals and public officers. Inevitably much depends on the implications of the particular statute, the subject of the dispute.

Appeal from a refusal to grant *mandamus* is possible, with leave, to the Court of Appeal (Civil division) and thence, again with leave, to the House of Lords.

(ii) *Prohibition.*—This prerogative order is issued by the Queen's Bench Divisional Court to prevent a court or tribunal of inferior standing from proceeding further in a case in excess of that court or tribunal's jurisdiction. The order is only appropriate whilst the case is in progress and before a decision is reached. Once the decision has been given there is nothing that the order can "prohibit".

An example of the issue of the order is the case of *R.* v. *Electricity Commissioners, Ex parte London Electricity Joint Committee Company (1920) Limited* (1924), where the Electricity Commissioners were stopped from proceeding with a scheme which was *"ultra vires"* for the supply of electricity.

The rules which apply to the issue of an order of prohibition also apply to the order of *certiorari* and this must be borne in mind in what follows: In practice the individual usually finds that the matter has actually been decided before he can bring his complaint to the courts and this is why applications for *certiorari* are so much more frequent than those for prohibition.

(iii) *Certiorari.*—This prerogative order also is issued by the Queen's Bench Divisional Court but its purpose is to have the decision of a court, tribunal, public body or public officer, brought before the divisional court to have its legality considered and, if necessary, to have the decision quashed.

The essential factor which must be shown if an application for the order is to be successful is that the person or body in question is under a duty to act judicially. The distinction here is between a judicial decision and an administrative decision, and it has already been seen how difficult it is to drawn the dividing line. If, however, the decision is held to be an administrative one then this order is not available. Examples of four such cases are:

Nakkuda Ali v. *Jayaratne* (1951). The controller of textiles in Ceylon was empowered to cancel a textile licence where he had "reasonable grounds to believe that any dealer is unfit to be allowed to continue as a dealer". The controller cancelled a licence and the person concerned failed in his application for *certiorari* because the controller's action was held to be administrative and not judicial.

R. v. *Metropolitan Police Commissioner, Ex parte Parker* (1953). The cancellation by the Police Commissioner of a taxi-driver's licence where the Commissioner was statutorily authorised to do so, provided he was satisfied that the holder was not a fit person to have such a licence, was held to be an administrative and not a judicial decision. This decision was reached despite the fact that the Commissioner did not give the taxi-driver the opportunity to appear before him or of presenting his case.

Ex parte Fry (1954). A fireman who had refused an order to clean a senior officer's uniform was duly cautioned as a matter of staff discipline. His attempt to have the disciplinary decision quashed by *certiorari* failed because the whole matter was held to be one of internal discipline, *i.e.* an administrative matter.

Vidyodaya University of Ceylon v. *Silva* (1964). The dismissed professor of a University in Ceylon attempted to obtain an order of *certiorari* to quash the decision to dismiss him. He was not successful because the court held that it would not use a prerogative order to deal with a dismissal under an ordinary contract of employment. The common characteristic of these cases is that the court would not intervene to assist the complainant on the basis indicated. However, when the decision is held to be a judicial or even a quasi-judicial one (*i.e.* having some substantial characteristics of a judicial decision) then the court may intervene to assist a complainant. The grounds on which this intervention may occur have been considered earlier in this chapter, *viz.* breach of the rules of natural justice, *"ultra vires"* action or error of law appearing on the face of the record. If the court is satisfied that it should intervene it will do so by way of the prerogative order of *certiorari*. To illustrate the position there follow a number of examples of successful applications for *certiorari*: the cases have been selected to show the various organisations against which the order has issued as well as the variety of circumstances involved.

(1) to quash the resolution of a local authority which had given a planning decision in which one of the members had a particular interest and on which he had spoken and cast a vote. This action by the member affected was not only a criminal offence but it was held to invalidate the decision of all the remaining members. (It is arguable how far this case should be relied on, particularly since later legislation has affected the whole field of planning law).

R. v. *Hendon Rural District Council, Ex parte Chorley* (1933)

(2) to quash the decision of an administrative tribunal where the determination of the body, a medical appeal tribunal, revealed an error of law on the face of the record.

Re Gilmore's Application (1957)

similarly where a medical appeal tribunal failed to observe the rules of natural justice in refusing to hear the reports of consultants for both sides in a case.

R. v. *Medical Appeal Tribunal (Midland Region), Ex parte Carrarini* (1966).

(3) to quash the decision of a central Government Minister, the Minister of Housing and Local Government, when his decision revealed an error of law. The Minister was required by statute to satisfy himself and then certify, that land had become "incapable of reasonably beneficial use in its existing state". Instead the Minister certified that the land was "substantially less useful". This was held not to satisfy the statute and to be an error of law on the face of the record.

R. v. *Minister of Housing and Local Government, Ex parte Chichester Rural District Council* (1960).

(4) to quash the decision of a legal aid committee which mistakenly allowed an application for legal aid. The applicant went bankrupt and his trustee in bankruptcy continued with the application for legal aid. The application was then granted based on the financial standing of the applicant. The defendant company objected to the grant of legal aid on this basis and obtained an order of *certiorari*.

R. v. *Manchester Legal Aid Committee, Ex parte R. A. Brand & Co., Ltd.* (1952).

(5) to quash the decision of magistrates where they improperly announced the conviction of a defendant for careless driving before he had been given the opportunity to present his defence in full.

Ex parte Bowgin (1965).

These examples which are nearly all of recent origin show the order of *certiorari* issuing against local authorities, administrative tribunals, magistrates, a central Government Minister, and a legal aid committee. In R. v. *Paddington Valuation Officer, Ex parte Peachey Property Corporation Ltd.* (1966) an application for the order was made to quash the valuation list which had been prepared by a civil servant. As it happened the court was not satisfied that the valuation officer in the case in question had erred, but they made it clear that if he had erred then the order would have issued to quash the valuation list. So *certiorari* could in the appropriate circumstances be issued against the decision of a civil servant, as well as against his minister. (See Appendix B).

As with *mandamus* the order of *certiorari* is discretionary and is not available where some other remedy is more appropriate; but whereas there is no fixed time limit in an application for *mandamus*, although obviously the court will wish to be satisfied that there has been no undue delay, in the case of *certiorari* a six month time limit from the date of the decision in question is strictly enforced. Also in both instances there is some little doubt about the standing required by the court of an application for the order, what is known as *"locus standi"* : in general terms it is clear that the court will consider an application from a person aggrieved, but whether an application by an unaffected by-stander would be accepted or not is arguable. A further point is that some of the procedural rules affecting the orders are of considerable antiquity and they do not assist the court in arriving at the truth: for example, cross-examination of a person swearing an affidavit is almost unheard of, and the court never orders the discovery of documents (both sides being forced to reveal all relevant documents). These procedural rules have led to the orders being much criticised.

Certiorari quashes the decision of the lower court or other body and this means that the proceedings will either cease altogether or will have to start all over again. The court will never substitute its own decision for that of the court or other body in question. This is one way in which the courts' role in the issue of a prerogative order is quite different from an appeal. No other remedy accompanies the grant of a prerogative order: it is thus not possible to claim damages in the same action with an application for a prerogative order.

The right to seek an order of *certiorari* can only be excluded by Parliament and then only by the most clear-cut statement. The court always works from the presumption that Parliament intends the judiciary to supervise the various bodies charged with taking decisions of a judicial nature. In many cases where Parliament has laid it down that the decision of the body or person in question was to be "final", the courts have interpreted this to mean "final on the facts of the case" and not "final on the law". This interpretation has been given further force by Parliament itself in the Tribunals and Inquiries Act 1958, section 11, which states that where in previous legislation the supervision of the courts appeared by the words used to be excluded, that such decisions should nonetheless be subject to examination and control in the courts by the orders of *mandamus* and *certiorari*.

Appeal from a refusal to grant the order of *certiorari* is possible, with leave, to the Court of Appeal (Civil Division) and thence, again with leave, to the House of Lords.

(b) Declaration and Injunction

(i) *The Declaratory Judgment.*—This is a modern remedy which, if the experience of the United States of America is a guide, will rapidly oust the prerogative orders as a judicial method of controlling administrative authorities. In what has been said about the prerogative orders it will have been apparent that there are many difficulties. The most significant is the difficulty of definition between what is a judicial and what is an administrative decision. Others may be summarised as the alternative remedy aspect; the question of who may make an application; the special position of the Crown in *mandamus*; and in *certiorari*, no discovery of documents and the six months' time limit.

The declaratory judgment avoids all these difficulties since being an equitable remedy it also is discretionary and it has none of the disadvantages which have been noticed. Its apparent disadvantage, that being only a declaration it has no coercive force, is not really a disadvantage when it is appreciated that all public authorities will abide by the court's decision. Since the Crown Proceedings Act 1947 a declaration is even possible against the Crown.

There are nonetheless limits to the willingness of the court to intervene. It will not settle hypothetical cases, such as in *Re Barnato deceased* (1949), when trustees desired to know whether or not estate duty would, in the future, be payable if they took a certain course. Again if some other remedy is possible it is unlikely that the court will proceed to a declaration. Likewise if an Act of Parliament makes it clear that a decision is to be given by a Minister, a declaration will not be made to alter that decision. For example in *Healey* v. *Minister of Health* (1955) the Minister decided, as he was authorised to do by statute, that Healey was not a mental health officer: the court would not make a declaration that the Minister was in error, since Parliament had given the power to make the decision to the minister and he had decided.

A declaratory judgment under the Rules of the Supreme Court is sought from one High Court judge. Because of this it is possible to claim for damages as well as seek a declaration in one action. A good example of such an action was *Vine* v. *National Dock Labour Board* (1957) where a docker claimed that his name had been improperly removed from the register of dock workers. He succeeded

in obtaining damages and also a declaration that his name should
be entered again on the register.

The sorts of situations in which declarations have been obtained
are diverse; the following summary of decided cases is intended
to show the range:

(1) dealing with an excess of jurisdiction by a local authority,
i.e. acting *"ultra vires"*. *Prescott* v. *Birmingham Corporation*
(1954) where the Corporation wished to reduce fares for
elderly persons using the municipal bus service and this was
declared to be *"ultra vires"*.

(2) dealing with the validity of conditions attached to a planning
permission. *Fawcett Properties* v. *Buckinghamshire County Council*
(1961).

(3) dealing with the calculation of legal aid under the Legal
Aid and Advice Act 1949. *Taylor* v. *National Assistance Board*
(1957).

(4) dealing with the validity of an expulsion from a trade
union. *Annamunthodo* v. *Oilfield Workers Trade Union* (1961),
and *Taylor* v. *National Union of Seamen* (1967).

(5) dealing with the legality of questions asked in a form issued
by the Inland Revenue. *Dyson* v. *Attorney-General* (1911).

(6) dealing with the dismissal of a chief constable. *Ridge* v.
Baldwin (1964).

Procedurally any private individual affected directly in the matter
may seek a declaration: if the individual is not himself affected
he will inform the Attorney-General who may then bring the action.
This is known as a "relator" action.

The result of the declaration will almost certainly be that the
public body concerned will comply with the court's decision.

(ii) *Injunction.*—An injunction is an equitable remedy and is
frequently obtained in private law particularly in the law of tort,
for example, to prevent the commission of a further trespass or
nuisance. In public law an injunction may be available to prevent,
for example, a local authority from spending money where it has no
legal power to do so, *i.e.* to prevent *"ultra vires"* expenditure.

An injunction is an order from the court, normally one High Court
judge, requiring the body concerned either not to do some particular
thing or requiring it to do some particular thing. Most injunctions
are to enforce a negative stipulation, *i.e.* they order the body not to
do something. Only an individual directly affected can apply to the
court for an injunction but someone who is only generally concerned

can inform the Attorney-General who can then bring the case "at the relation of" the individual. The value of the injunction as an order is that any failure to observe it is a contempt of court punishable by severe sanctions including imprisonment.

The obtaining of injunctions against administrative bodies is not widespread. Occasionally one will issue against a local authority but a particular qualification to this remedy is that it is not possible to obtain an injunction directed to the Crown or its servants (s. 21 (1) Crown Proceedings Act 1947). This is one reason why the declaration is more in use since it can be obtained in an action where the Crown is a party.

A good example of a case in which an injunction was issued to restrain an administrative body from an *"ultra vires"* action is the *Attorney-General* v. *Fulham Corporation* (1921). In this case the Corporation wished to provide a laundry service for its ratepayers. It could point to statutory authority to provide wash-houses but not to actually do the work by its own employees, i.e. provide a laundry. An injunction was issued, presumably at the relation of a local laundry-owner, to restrain the corporation from providing the laundry service. It is possible to obtain an injunction and some other remedy in one and the same action; for example, a trade union member who alleges that he has been wrongfully expelled from his union may be able to claim successfully (i) an injunction to prevent his expulsion, and (ii) damages for loss of employment sustained while the case was pending.

A further use of an injunction is on the application of some administrative body which finds its powers in law inadequate to achieve the remedy it needs. In *Attorney-General (ex. rel. Manchester Corporation)* v. *Harris* (1961), the court granted an injunction to restrain the defendants from continuing to sell flowers in contravention of an Act under which they had been summoned and convicted some 237 times. The penalty under the Act was clearly an inadequate deterrent. On a somewhat similar basis in *Attorney-General (ex rel. Egham Urban District Council)* v. *Smith* (1958) the court granted an injunction to restrain the defendant from flouting the planning legislation whereby he used some of his land for caravan sites and made various applications for planning approval which he knew would be refused.

From what has been said it will be plain that whilst the remedy of a court injunction is a useful one in certain circumstances, in practice it is not as frequently sought as applications for the prerogative orders or a declaration.

(c) Habeas Corpus and an Action for Damages

(i) *Habeas corpus.*—The ancient prerogative writ of *habeas corpus* remains available as a method by which a court can require the detention of a named individual to be justified by the detaining body. The writ is so called because its opening words in Latin "*habeas corpus*" mean "you have the body"; and it is directed to the person detaining the "body" in question, to produce it to the Court issuing the writ, in order that it may examine the legality of the detention. The writ will issue on the application of the person detained or by someone on his behalf. It may be issued by the Queen's Bench Divisional Court or by a High Court judge acting alone. Because of its importance in relation to personal liberty an application for *habeas corpus* takes precedence over all business before the court.

The normal process is for the court to issue the writ "*nisi*" which requires the detainer to bring the person detained before the court and there to show cause why the order of release should not be made "absolute", *i.e.* to justify the detention.

If the application arises from a civil matter an appeal against a refusal to grant the writ lies to the Court of Appeal (Civil division) and thence, with leave, to the House of Lords.

If the application arises from a criminal matter an appeal against a refusal to grant the writ lies direct from the Queen's Bench Divisional Court, with leave, to the House of Lords. The Administration of Justice Act 1960 which extended the appeal position introduced one controversial factor in that either side can appeal and it is thus possible for a detainee to win in the divisional court but lose in the House of Lords.

An interesting example of a successful application for *habeas corpus* occurred in *R. v. Governor of Wormwood Scrubs Prison, Ex parte Boydell* (1948) in which a former Army Officer had been arrested after his release and tried by court martial for offences alleged to have been committed whilst a serving officer. The Queen's Bench Divisional Court held that as he had been released from the service the applicant was no longer subject to military law and his conviction and punishment by the court martial would not be allowed to stand.

Although the number of applications for *habeas corpus* is few, the existence of the writ is a salutary warning to all those public officers and bodies who are responsible for taking away an individual's right to liberty.

(ii) *Action for Damages.*—It may be possible for an individual who has suffered some personal loss as a result of action by an administrative body to bring a claim for damages based in contract or tort, as appropriate, against that body.

Public bodies are just as liable for damages if they enter into a contract and then break it as is a private individual in those circumstances. Public bodies can make contracts quite freely for the conduct of their activities, and the general rule, now to be found in the Corporate Bodies Contracts Act 1960, is that such bodies can make contracts just like a private individual.

The liability of public bodies in tort is largely brought about by the doctrine of vicarious liability, under which the "servants" of such bodies who commit torts within the course of their employment, make their employing body, or "master", liable to the injured party, as well as being themselves liable. For instance negligent driving by a local authority refuse lorry driver resulting in injury to person or property will mean that in addition to the driver himself being liable, the local authority also will be liable. The result thus is that any public body can be liable, through its employees, for virtually any tort. The one defence which is of particular consequence here is that where Parliament has expressly authorised the body to do, whatever it is that is complained of as a tort, then the body can plead in defence "statutory authority". The defence will only suceed, however, where the body has acted expressly in compliance with its authority.

Whilst an Act of Parliament may sometimes provide a public body with a defence, it may also do the reverse and by placing a specific duty on the body make it liable to a private individual who suffers particular loss because of the failure of the body to carry out that duty. For example, in *Read* v. *Croydon Corporation* (1938) the corporation in breach of their statutory duty failed to provide pure water to their ratepayers. The plaintiff suffered financial loss as a result of his daughter contracting typhoid from the un-pure water supply. It was held that the plaintiff could successfully recover his loss for breach of statutory duty, and his daughter could successfully claim in negligence also. It should be added by way of caution that the right to sue for breach of statutory duty is hedged around with a number of restrictions; often the statute itself specifically provides a remedy and this may indirectly prevent a claim for damages. Also it is only a person who can point to particular loss, who will have any prospect of succeeding in a claim, and even here he will only do so provided the statute expressly or impliedly envisages the claim.

4 OTHER METHODS OF CHALLENGING ACTION BY ADMINISTRATIVE BODIES

The preceding section has been entirely concerned with the actual methods which the courts may use to control the actions of administrative bodies. Because the foregoing emphasis has been on judicial remedies it must not be overlooked, however, that there are various other ways in which the activities of these bodies can be called in question.

(a) Parliamentary Control

As the supreme power in the State, Parliament can always pass legislation to change the law as previously laid down, and this can extend to the abolition of any of the administrative bodies with whose services Parliament is dissatisfied. Far less drastic is the supervision which Parliament normally extends to the work of the administration: the Parliamentary question to a minister, the work of the select committee on statutory instruments, the annual report of the council on tribunals, the work of the select committee on the nationalised industries, the annual reports of ministers laid before Parliament—each one of these in its own way and quite exclusive of the control exercised through the courts, is a check on possible abuse of power by an administrative body. To this control must be added the pressure of back-bench Members of Parliament with their letters to, and interviews with, ministers and the wide-scale publicity given by the Press and broadcasting bodies to any alleged abuse of power by an administrative body.

(b) The Ombudsman

The latest addition to the methods of challenging the actions of administrative bodies is the appointment by the Parliamentary Commissioner Act 1967 of the Parliamentary Commissioner for Administration or as he is frequently called, after the Scandinavian parallel, the Ombudsman. This official is intended to carry out investigations into allegations of maladministration against central government departments. He will be a civil servant but like the judges will be dismissable only by petition of both Houses of Parliament to the Queen. To begin with he will not be concerned with complaints about local authorities nor about public corporations, but the committee which recommended his appointment foresaw the likelihood of his terms of reference being widened ultimately. At present he can act only on complaints which have been submitted to him through a Member of Parliament, and the powers which he has been given have been heavily criticised in that there is a wide range of matters which he is not permitted to investigate. These include such matters as: national security, foreign affairs, administration of colonies, criminal law cases, and personnel matters in the civil service and the armed forces. Even in those matters which he may investigate restrictions have been placed on the documents to which he may have access. Another possible difficulty is the likelihood of a collision of responsibility between the Parliamentary Commissioner and the Council on Tribunals. Whilst the position of the Parliamentary Commissioner looks anything but promising, judgment will have to be reserved to await developments.

Chapter 6

Liberties of the Subject

1 INTRODUCTION

In a sense this is the most important topic in a study of the subject "public law". There can be no more important matter than the right of each individual to enjoy complete liberty. However, there are and must be limits to this freedom. Important though it is that there shall be no arbitrary arrest and detention it is nonetheless true that in any developed civilisation the freedom of the individual is hedged about by many restrictions. Anyone with the necessary money may purchase a car. Only a driver who has passed the statutory driving test may drive that car on a highway. This is a restriction on the liberty of the purchaser of the car but few would deny the need for the restriction. Today legislative restrictions of this kind are growing in number annually. A man buys a piece of land. The local planning authority is the body which will decide what use he can make of that land. He may wish to build a bungalow but the planning authority may indirectly insist that he build a house: what is more they will require to approve the detailed plan of the house and may even tell him the colour of the tiles he must put on the roof. This clearly is a very real restriction on the liberty of the purchaser of the land to do what he wishes with his own: but this restriction is imposed in the interests of the community and few would quarrel with the need for some planning restrictions. The most important restriction of all is that the freedom to do what one likes with what one earns is affected by legislation which takes away from the apparent amount earned, income tax, contributions to the national insurance scheme and contributions to the national pensions scheme.

The one consolation to be derived from this state of affairs is that every one of these restrictions has been authorised in the fullest detail by Parliament and can thus be taken to have the general approval of the community.

147

This introduction began by saying that the liberty of the subject is, in a sense, the most important topic in a study of public law. It would perhaps be relevant to conclude by pointing out that throughout the preceding five chapters the underlying object is to see how law affecting the public is made and to see also how the individual member of the public is protected against an abuse of power by any of the law making agencies. The legislation made by Parliament can be theoretically checked by the democratic process of election, by the hostile Parliamentary question and by the pressure of public opinion through the Press and broadcasting: the very different law-making powers of the judges are subject to a wide system of appeals and in the last resort to being over-ridden by a new Act of Parliament: in the case of delegated legislation and the decisions of administrative tribunals, ministers, local authorities and public corporations the various grounds on which the courts will intervene are now reasonably apparent and so are the methods by which this intervention will be made effective. This then is what this book on public law has been about and when all this has been taken into account what is left for consideration is this final chapter, the liberty of the subject.

In the sections which follow, the liberties of the subject will be examined under the headings—right to personal freedom, right to hold public meetings, rights over property, freedom of speech and finally a survey will be made of some important qualifications to these liberties.

2 RIGHT TO PERSONAL FREEDOM

English law has long attached great importance to the right of every individual to enjoy his existence free from the risk of arbitrary detention. Any person whose liberty has been wrongfully taken away may apply to the High Court for the issue of a writ of *habeas corpus* (see chapter 5). This writ requires the gaoler to bring the person named before the High Court immediately, and an application for the writ takes precedence over any other business before the court. The number of applications for the issue of the writ annually is quite small but its very existence is a major safeguard against abuse.

(a) The power to arrest

(i) *Criminal Law Act 1967.*—The power to arrest an individual in English law is very limited. Such a power resides almost as much in the ordinary private citizen as it does in the police, although in practice the matter is usually left to the police. Until the recent abolition of the distinction between felonies and misdemeanours a private citizen could arrest for a treason, felony or dangerous wounding committed in his presence; or he could arrest a person whom he reasonably suspected of committing such an offence provided the offence had actually been committed. A police officer had exactly the same power to arrest, with the added advantage that he could arrest on reasonable suspicion even if it later turned out that no treason, felony or dangerous wounding had been committed. It is however proper to add at this point that a police officer had, and still has, special statutory powers of arrest in some circumstances.

Under the Criminal Law Act 1967, which was passed on July 11, 1967 the distinction between treason, felony and misdemeanour was abolished. Instead the crimes for which a private citizen or a police officer can arrest are given the new rather unhelpful title of "arrestable offences". Such offences are defined in the Act as those for which a person could be sentenced to five years' imprisonment or more. All other offences are known as "non-arrestable offences". This means that a private citizen or police officer can arrest for an arrestable offence committed in his presence, or on reasonable suspicion when such an offence has actually been committed. A police officer will retain the added advantage that he can arrest on reasonable suspicion even if it later turns out that no arrestable offence has been committed. The new Act does not affect the special statutory powers of arrest which police officers have in defined circumstances.

If a private citizen does make an arrest he must bring the person arrested before a police officer or magistrate in order to make the charge as soon as he reasonably can. A police officer making an arrest has a wider discretion in that he can, if he thinks fit, pursue his investigations in a reasonable way for a matter of hours before taking the person arrested into formal custody.

(ii) *No detention without arrest.*—The power to arrest then, as has been shown, is clearly very limited and it must be stressed that the person arrested must be told at the time of his arrest the offence with which he is charged. There is no power to detain a person without arresting him. A police officer may invite a person to accompany him to the police station to help him with his inquiries but the person concerned need not go, and even if he does go, he is entitled to leave at any time.

E.P.L.—6*

The case of *Rice* v. *Connolly* (1966) has again served to emphasise the very real difficulty of the police when dealing with the uncooperative citizen. In this case a police officer saw Rice behaving suspiciously in the early hours of the morning in an area where breaking offences had that night occurred. Rice refused to answer any questions, would not give his full name and address and would not agree to accompany the police officer to a police box for identification purposes. He said "If you want me, you will have to arrest me", whereupon he was arrested and charged with wilfully obstructing the police officer in the execution of his duty. It was admitted by the police that Rice had no connection with the breakings. His appeal against conviction was unanimously allowed by the Queen's Bench Divisional Court. Lord Chief Justice PARKER said "It seems to me quite clear that though every citizen has a moral duty, or if you like a social duty to assist the police, there is no legal duty to that effect, and indeed the whole basis of the common law is that right of the individual to refuse to answer questions put to him by persons in authority, and a refusal to accompany those in authority to any particular place, short, of course, of arrest". Mr Justice MARSHALL put his view of the matter more succinctly; "In order to uphold this conviction it appears to me that one has to assent to the proposition that where a citizen is acting merely within his legal rights he is thereby committing a criminal offence."

(b) Bail

There is no restriction before trial on the liberty of an individual charged with a summary offence but the punishment can, although it rarely does, involve imprisonment. Even where the charge is an indictable offence it is usual for bail to be arranged pending trial. The system of bail in force requires the accused person to furnish guarantors prepared to provide a sum of money as security that he will stand trial. Only in the most serious cases is it usual for the accused person to be kept in custody pending trial and even then he must be brought publicly before a magistrate every eight days to be remanded. For this reason the prosecution are expected to prepare their case for the earliest possible hearing. In any case the accused person has a right of appeal against the magistrates' refusal to grant bail to a High Court judge sitting in chambers.

(c) Wrongful arrest

If a private citizen or a police officer makes a mistake and arrests the wrong person, or arrests in circumstances which do not justify an arrest, he may be sued in civil law for damages for the tort of false imprisonment. If the arrest was totally unjustified it is even possible that he may also be liable for the tort of malicious prosecution. The case of *Christie* v. *Leachinsky* (1947) is revealing of the risks which police officers run in making an arrest. In that case police officers arrested a man for being in unlawful possession of certain goods, being a statutory offence for which they had no such power of arrest. The next morning that charge was withdrawn and larceny was substituted. On a claim for damages for false imprisonment the House of Lords held that the claim succeeded for the one night's unlawful detention, so reinforcing the principle that, as Lord SIMONDS said, "a man is not to be deprived of his liberty except in due course and process of law". The vital factor is that the person making the arrest must immediately inform the person arrested of the criminal charge which is to be brought against him. In order for the arrest to be justified the charge must be one which allows for an arrest to be made. This was the point of the *Christie* v. *Leachinsky* case.

The Police Act 1964, section 48, has clarified the legal responsibility of the Police Authority for any civil wrong done by police officers. That section states that "The chief officer of police for any police area shall be liable in respect of torts committed by constables under his direction and control in the performance or purported performance of their functions in like manner as a master is liable in respect of torts committed by his servants in the course of their employment, and accordingly shall in respect of any such tort be treated for all purposes as a joint tortfeasor". Thus, through the chief constable, the police fund of the local authority is available to meet the damages awarded against a police officer. Prior to the 1964 Police Act the position was very confused and unsatisfactory, since neither the Crown nor the local authority were technically regarded as "the master" of a police officer, and until that Act the claim had to be made against the police officer concerned in his personal capacity and he might not have the means to meet the claim. *Fisher* v. *Oldham Corporation* (1930) was the leading case until the 1964 Police Act. In that case the Oldham Police wrongly arrested an innocent man. His claim against the Oldham Corporation failed because it was held that the police were not the servants or agents of the corporation.

The only grounds on which a police officer can feel completely at ease that the arrest he is making is sound in law is where he is executing a warrant obtained from and signed by a magistrate. In such a case he is acting ministerially under the instructions of a judicial officer and as such he cannot himself be successfully sued. The magistrate will only issue a warrant for arrest on a sworn information, that is a statement made on oath before him, and the warrant must name a specific person, so that generally there is not much chance of a mistake being made.

(d) The Judges' Rules (See Appendix C)

Personal liberty is so highly valued in England that the respect for it governs not only the law with regard to arrest but extends to the various rules of evidence and procedure which protect an accused person both before and at his trial. As soon as an arrest has been made by a police officer he must observe certain rules known as the Judges' Rules, which deal with the taking of statements from persons under arrest. These rules which have been laid down by the Queen's Bench Division judges as guidance for the police have come to be observed as if they were statutorily enacted. Hence a police officer must immediately caution the person arrested in the following terms: "Do you wish to say anything? You are not obliged to say anything unless you wish to do so but whatever you say will be taken down in writing and may be given in evidence." Any statement or confession obtained from the accused person by a police officer in contravention of the Judges' Rules is not likely to be admitted in evidence at the trial. The rules thus curb any tendency on the part of the police to obtain a statement at all costs and by any means. Similarly the various presumptions which the court makes in relation to the accused at his trial are all aimed at giving the individual his liberty; for example:

(a) the accused is innocent until proved guilty by the prosecution beyond all reasonable doubt

(b) the accused may plead "not guilty" and thereafter remain totally silent throughout the trial

(c) the accused's previous criminal record is not given to the court until after he has been convicted.

All these rules benefit the accused person very considerably and make the prosecution task more difficult.

A further protection for the accused is that where he is charged with an indictable offence he is entitled to be tried by a jury of twelve of his fellow citizens. Previously the jury's verdict had to be unanimous but by the Criminal Justice Act 1967 now law a majority verdict, where there are not more than two in the minority, may be accepted. Even after sentence the prisoner can appeal to a higher court in the hope of having the conviction quashed or the sentence reduced.

It is the intention then, that only after a carefully conducted trial, and, in serious cases, conviction by an unbiased jury, can any person in this country be deprived of his liberty.

One major qualification to this state of affairs is that in time of national emergency the executive obtains from the legislature extraordinary powers which allow for (*inter alia*) detention without trial as expedient in the interest of the State. Although the courts in acknowledging the supremacy of Parliament have had to uphold such powers, they have done so with considerable and openly expressed misgivings and generally in the result there has been little cause for complaint in the executive's actual use of the powers.

Two minor qualifications are first the law's recognition of the right of parental control over children and second the law in relation to the detention of the mentally ill. Both are quite clear qualifications and both are fully justifiable on reasonable grounds: conduct which, it was alleged, exceeded the bounds of reasonableness could be challenged by an application for a writ of *habeas corpus*. The detention would then have to be justified to the court.

3 RIGHT TO HOLD PUBLIC MEETINGS

(a) Inadequate provisions

The law on the subject of public meetings is far from straightforward. First of all it can be said that there is no legal right for any group of persons to hold a public meeting. On the other hand there is no law which stops them from holding a public meeting.

The major difficulty is one of place. There is no place where public meetings can be held as of right. Despite public opinion to the contrary, Speakers Corner and Trafalgar Square in London are not freely available on demand to any group which wishes to hold a public meeting. Always, wherever the place, the consent of some person or some organisation will be necessary.

Local authorities have the same right of control over the premises owned by them as have private owners and this control extends as much to their parks and open spaces as to actual buildings. Only in the case of a general election is there a right to demand the use of local authority premises and this is limited to meetings organised by a candidate in the election subject to the payment of a reasonable fee. It is thus apparent that no public meeting can be held on local authority premises or land without the express consent of the council.

(b) Meeting on the highway

Nor does the law recognise any right to hold a public meeting on the highway. The legal theory is that a highway has been dedicated by the owners of the land over which the highway runs for the purpose of public passage, or as the old legal term has it, for egress and regress. Thus any person who uses it for any other purpose commits the civil wrong of trespass and probably the criminal offence of obstructing the highway. Examples of the civil wrong are seen in *Harrison* v. *Duke of Rutland* (1893) and *Hickman* v. *Maisey* (1900). In the former case Harrison was held to be a trespasser when interrupting the Duke of Rutland's shooting parties by misusing the highway. It seems that Harrison stood on the highway opening and shutting his umbrella to warn the game away. In the latter case a journalist tipster was also held to be a trespasser on the highway when he had been standing on the highway timing race-horses exercising nearby. An explanation of the criminal law aspect is to be found in *Arrowsmith* v. *Jenkins* (1963) where a young lady who held a meeting on the highway was successfully prosecuted under s. 121 (1) of the Highways Act 1959. That section reads:

"If a person, without lawful authority or excuse, in any way wilfully obstructs the free passage along a highway he shall be guilty of an offence and shall be liable in respect thereof to a fine not exceeding forty shillings."

The obstruction in the case in question was substantial since for five minutes the highway was completely blocked. It is then from these cases quite apparent that no public meeting can be held on the highway as of right.

(c) Processions

Another form of public meeting, the procession, is subject to even more stringent controls. A procession, because it involves movement on the highway, is not a trespass but is much more likely to be caught by the criminal law obstruction provisions of the Highways Act. The risk of obstruction is self-evident and by s. 3 (1) of the Public Order Act 1936 a chief officer of police can, if he reasonably apprehends a breach of the peace, control the route of a procession and impose other conditions designed to prevent public disorder. By the following subsection processions can, in boroughs and urban districts, be prohibited completely for up to three months subject to the consent of a Secretary of State and of the local council. Provision is also made for a similar prohibition in London. The right to hold a public meeting in the form of a procession is then very much restricted. It would appear to depend entirely on obtaining the goodwill of the local police.

(d) Prevention of breaches of the peace

This statement of the strict legal position concerning public meetings is however to over-emphasise the theory at the expense of what actually happens. In practice many thousands of public meetings take place every year and no police officer would dream of even attending, let alone interfering in, the vast majority of them. On analysis it is not difficult to see that the main consideration is the need to maintain law and order and to prevent breaches of the peace. Naturally the police are the interested parties on this account and it has become customary to rely on their good sense and judgment in this field of public law. There is an obvious danger in leaving such a discretion to any person or organisation in that the discretion may come to be exercised for the convenience of the person or organisation concerned rather than in the public interest. However the glare of publicity, in which at the present time situations, which involve the maintenance of order, arise and are handled, is probably in itself an adequate form of protection against abuse of power.

The leading cases in this branch of the law, without being particularly revealing, all point to the concern of the courts in preventing breaches of the peace. The earliest case *Beatty* v. *Gillbanks* (1882) concerned Salvation Army processions in Weston-super-Mare which consistently resulted in violence at the hands of an opposing group calling itself the Skeleton Army. The Salvation Army although requested not to hold processions continued to do so and their leaders were charged with unlawful assembly. On appeal, a conviction by the magistrates was quashed on the grounds that the unlawfulness of the assembly was the result of the conduct of the Skeleton Army and therefore the prosecution had been instituted against the wrong group.

In *Wise* v. *Dunning* (1902) a magistrates' order binding over a Protestant "Crusader" to keep the peace was upheld by a divisional court of the Queen's Bench Division. The person concerned had deliberately set out to give offence to the Roman Catholic population in Liverpool and had on previous occasions by his provocative words and conduct caused breaches of the peace to take place. The divisional court held that the binding over order was perfectly proper and appropriate in the circumstances.

In *Duncan* v. *Jones* (1936) the police were successful in their prosecution of a woman for the offence of obstructing a police officer in the execution of his duty when she refused to move a meeting she was holding, away from the entrance to a training institution for the unemployed. On a previous occasion the meeting had caused an outbreak of violence in the premises and the police, having grounds for fearing a recurrence of the trouble, insisted that the meeting be held elsewhere. The divisional court upheld the conviction.

Another case of more recent date is *Chandler* v. *Director of Public Prosecutions* (1964) where an organisation, the Committee of 100, in its efforts to persuade the nation to agree to a policy of nuclear disarmament held a demonstration intended to immobilise an air base for some six hours. The prosecution was brought under s. 1 of the Official Secrets Act 1911 and Chandler and others were convicted and sentenced to terms of imprisonment. The section in question makes it an offence for any person to approach or enter a prohibited place for any purpose prejudicial to the safety of the State. Attention is drawn to this case because it shows how the maintenance of law and order in relation to the holding of public meetings can, when the Government so decides, be enforced by the use of very rigorous statutory provisions. No one would have anticipated when the 1911 Act was passed that a section intended to cover spying would be invoked in the circumstances of a non-violent demonstration. Even so the House of Lords were unanimous in upholding the conviction.

The cases are not easy and aspects of them have been much criticised, but what is constant to all of them is the emphasis which is placed on the maintenance of law and order.

(e) Police attendance at meetings

In the actual conduct of a meeting the law again will only interfere to prevent a possible breach of the peace. The vast majority of public meetings are held without any need for the presence of the police: this is quite natural since it is only in the very rare case that the possibility of a breach of the peace arises. The leading case on the subject is *Thomas* v. *Sawkins* (1935) where police officers insisted on attending an advertised public meeting despite having been asked to leave. The divisional court of the Queen's Bench Division held that where the police apprehended a possible breach of the peace as a result of the meeting they were fully entitled to attend and they could not be forced to leave. Lord Chief Justice HEWART said:

> "I am not at all prepared to accept the doctrine that it is only where an offence has been, or is being, committed, that the police are entitled to enter and remain on private premises. On the contrary it seems to me that a police officer has *ex virtute officii* full right so to act when he has reasonable ground for believing that an offence is imminent or is likely to be committed."

(f) Public Order Act 1936

A further useful statutory provision which enables the police to deal with misconduct at a meeting is to be found in s. 5 of the Public Order Act 1936. This lays down that:

> "any person who in any public place or at any public meeting uses threatening, abusive or insulting words or behaviour with intent to provoke a breach of the peace or whereby a breach of the peace is likely to be occasioned shall be guilty of an offence."

The Public Order Act 1936 was intended to assist the police in maintaining law and order in the difficult days of the 1930's when violent clashes between the Fascists and the Communists at their public meetings became common. The Act has proved useful in somewhat similar circumstances in more recent years as is seen in the case of *Jordan* v. *Burgoyne* (1963). At a meeting in Trafalgar Square, Jordan, the National Socialist leader, having deliberately insulted the many opponents in his audience, developed in his speech the theme that "Hitler was right" and in so doing created complete disorder. The divisional court of the Queen's Bench Division had no hesitation in finding that he had committed an offence under s. 5 of the 1936 Act. Stress was laid on the title of the Act, "it is a Public Order Act" and this emphasis on the need to preserve public order at public meetings is in keeping with all that has gone before. Lord Chief Justice PARKER explained the balance between freedom of speech and the offence charged in this way:

> "A man is entitled to express his views as strongly as he likes, to criticise his opponents, to say disagreeable things about his opponents and about their policies, and to do anything of that sort. But what he must not do is—and these are the words of the section—he must not threaten, he must not be abusive and he must not insult them, 'insult' in the sense of 'hit by

words'. It seems to me that this is a perfectly clear case and that the defendant was guilty of the offence charged."

(g) Race Relations Act 1965

The latest development in this vexed field is the passing of the Race Relations Act 1965. Section 1 of this Act makes it a criminal offence to exercise racial discrimination in a place of public resort and s. 6 of the Act makes it a criminal offence to stir up hatred against any section of the public in Great Britain distinguished by colour, race or ethnic or national origins. The offence is committed by the publication or distribution of written matter or by the use of threatening, abusive or insulting words. As a further measure s. 7 of the Act extends the provisions of s. 5 of the Public Order Act 1936 to cover the publication or distribution of written matter.

4   RIGHT OF ASSOCIATION

Linked with the right to hold a public meeting is the right for individuals freely to join together to associate for some purpose which they see as being for their mutual benefit. It may be for business purposes as in the case of a partnership, or to protect or improve their conditions of employment as in the case of a trade union, or it may be for leisure activities like forming a golf club or the formation of a religious society.

In general terms the law will allow individuals to form such associations quite freely provided that their activities do not involve an unlawful object. Such organisations do not have any special legal status but their identity consists of all the members and so if a claim is brought against a partnership or a golf club, all the partners and all the members of the club are, generally, liable. This means that the individuals who join such an association do themselves in their personal capacity obtain rights and undertake liabilities.

Certain forms of association have by Act of Parliament been given a special status known as corporate status. Examples of such bodies are local authorities and limited liability companies. Here the individuals who form the association do not remain liable in their personal capacity for the activities of the association. Under the Act of Parliament the association has been given a separate legal personality of its own. This distinction between associations which have no separate legal personality and those which have, is technically known as the difference between an unincorporated association and a corporation. Hence a golf club is an unincorporated association whilst a limited liability company is a corporation.

All associations fall, with one exception only, into one of these two groups. The exception is a trade union. For reasons of history the combination of workmen to protect their own interests and to improve their working conditions was long regarded as undesirable, and, at one stage, as criminal. Over the last one hundred years trade unions have gradually been afforded recognition by Act of Parliament as lawful associations and their individual members have been given protection against actions in contract or tort when acting collectively. Nonetheless a trade union is neither an unincorporated association nor a corporation.

One specific qualification to this freedom to associate is to be found in the Public Order Act 1936 which attempts to curb the establishment of quasi-military organisations and so prohibits the wearing of uniforms and displays of physical force for political objects.

5 RIGHTS OVER PROPERTY

"The Englishman's home is his castle." This maxim has for long been a boast in England but it is necessary to consider how far it remains true.

The fact is that today Parliament can and does pass legislation which over and over again makes nonsense of the maxim. A recent newspaper report told of a householder being prosecuted because he failed to permit a public health inspector to enter his premises for the purpose of inspection, pending the future clearance of the property as being unfit for human habitation. The householder claimed "that the Englishman's home is his castle" and was fined for his pains.

Similarly owners are required to give access to gas, electricity, water, post office telephone and other employees of public service undertakings if they wish to use the service which is in question. Even if one does not wish to use the service there is a possibility that by statutory authority a telegraph pole can be put in, or mains services under, one's garden however much objection is taken.

The general rule, however, is that an occupier is free to permit or refuse access to his property at his discretion. This is particularly important in relation to police powers of entry and search. Just as the power of arrest is hedged around with limitations so also the right of a policeman to enter and search premises is very limited. If a policeman obtains a search warrant from a magistrate he is then entitled to enter and carry out a search of premises but before the magistrate issues such a warrant he will wish to be satisfied that there are reasonable grounds for permitting a search to be made. The power to grant such warrants is specifically given by a number of statutes to magistrates and in the case of the Public Order Act 1936 is given to a judge of the High Court. Always the warrant must name specific premises. A general warrant is illegal. This very important rule was laid down in *Entick* v. *Carrington* (1765) when a Secretary of State had to pay damages after issuing a general warrant to seize a person and his books and papers simply because the Government were anxious to suppress a seditious publication. Lord Chief Justice CAMDEN had no hesitation in declaring that such action was a trespass and in demolishing the argument that the seizure could be justified by the plea of state necessity. "The common law does not understand that kind of reasoning" he said.

The case of *Elias* v. *Pasmore* (1934) has, however, thrown some doubt on the position with regard to search. In that case the police entered the offices of an organisation in order to make an arrest under a warrant. They arrested the person concerned and then seized a number of documents which were in the offices. Some of the documents were used at the trial of the man arrested, others were returned, and others again were used in another prosecution. On a claim for damages, a judge at first instance held that the police were entitled on the arrest to search and seize any documents which might be evidence against the person arrested and further to seize any documents which revealed the commission of a crime by anyone else. The judge whilst allowing limited damages for the seizure of the documents not used at the trials and for the unlawful detention of documents after the conclusion of the trials, in one unfortunate phrase excused the seizure as being "in the interests of the state". The judgment has been much criticised and it is probably not wise to rely too much on it. In general terms the position remains that the police can only enter premises for search purposes either by consent of the owner or on a warrant properly issued under legal authority by a magistrate. Although this position is true of the police it must be admitted that a number of recent statutes have given limited powers to civil servants, local government officers and public corporation employees to enter private premises. In every case such entry is deemed by Parliament to be in the general public interest. Factory inspectors for instance and public health inspectors, fire officers, gas and electricity board inspectors all have such power for their professional purposes, but few would feel that intrusion by such officers in pursuance of their particular duty is really a breach of privacy or an abuse of power.

Whatever the theory, in practice, considerable respect is attached in England to the possession of land. Any unlawful interference with some-one else's land is technically a trespass to land and actionable as a tort. Despite the layman's view that trespass is permissible provided no actual damage is done, the fact is that any such trespass is, technically, actionable without proof of damage and the occupier is entitled to eject the trespasser provided only reasonable force is used. In the case of *Davis* v. *Lisle* (1936) a police officer, who entered premises to make enquiries about a summary offence and was ordered to leave, became a trespasser when he did not go. The occupier was thus entitled to eject him. The case turned on the point that the police officer had no legal right to enter the premises in the first place. It is in this tort of trespass to land that the protection which the law gives to the ownership and occupation of land is most clearly evident. This protection extends to prevent, under the law of nuisance in tort, any substantial interference with the enjoyment of property. Hence undue noise or discomfort from fumes emanating from nearby property may well be stopped by an injunction.

These rights in an owner or occupier are however balanced by duties imposed by law. The law of nuisance which bestows a legal right, also, as a corollary, bestows a legal duty, which is that one can enjoy one's own property but not so as to affect adversely an adjoining owner's enjoyment of his property. Also the occupier of property is forced to undertake a special responsibility under the Occupiers' Liability Act 1957. This Act lays down that an occupier may be liable to a visitor who suffers an injury as a result of the unsatisfactory state of the premises. Thus the ownership and occupation of property have both rights and liabilities attaching to it.

A further consideration is the extent to which Parliament has interfered with the right of an owner or an occupier to enjoy his property. In time of emergency the right of the Crown to seize privately owned property for the defence of the realm has long been acknowledged. Desperate cases invite desperate remedies. But it is harder to justify the parliamentary interference which has vested petrol and coal under the land in the Crown and which has consistently intervened in recent years in the right of an owner to use land as an investment. The landlord and tenant relationship has been so hedged about with statutory restrictions that the law on the subject is now intelligible only to specialists.

Furthermore in the last twenty years two major statutory developments have arisen which affect very substantially the freedom to enjoy property. The law with regard to town and country planning has now reached the stage where virtually no new use can be made of property without permission from some governmental body, in this case local planning authorities, being necessary. Control is very nearly complete and extends to the most minute detail.

The second development is the extension of the statutory power of compulsory purchase. It is true that the use of such a power by a local authority has to have the consent of the appropriate central Government department and that compensation has to be paid, but the scale of this development, since compulsory purchase can be exercised for practically all the functions of a local authority, does nevertheless reveal the fundamental limitations which exist in the field of the freedom to enjoy one's property. After all it only needs a confirmed compulsory purchase order to bring about the demolition of the Englishman's Castle!

The latest legislation on this topic, the Land Commission Act 1967 makes the matter considerably more pertinent. The Commission established under the Act has far more comprehensive powers of compulsory purchase than any previously possessed in peacetime by any Government body.

6 FREEDOM OF SPEECH

A person is free to say what he likes subject only to a number of well understood legal restrictions.

The most important restriction is that he shall not exercise this freedom to the detriment, without justification, of the reputation of another person. If he does, he commits the tort of defamation and he may be sued for damages accordingly. Defamation takes one of two forms. Libel which is generally written and therefore a permanent injury; or slander which is generally spoken and therefore a temporary injury. Defamation itself is defined as "the publication of an untrue statement which tends to lower a person's reputation in the estimation of right thinking members of society." The essence of the wrong is the unjustifiable injury to reputation and the damages awarded will be intended to compensate the injured party for the wrong done to his reputation. Certain defences are possible, the main elements of which are: justification—that the statement made is true in all material particulars. Absolute privilege—where for reasons of public policy complete freedom of speech is permitted such as in court proceedings and in parliamentary debates. Qualified privilege—where again for public policy reasons, freedom of speech is permitted, but this defence is not effective if it can be shown that malice entered into the making of the defamatory statement. Fair comment on a matter of public interest—where the publication of criticism of such matters as theatrical performances or football matches is held to be protected provided the criticism is limited to comment and that the subject matter can be said to be of public interest. Offer of amends—where by the Defamation Act 1952, s. 4 it is open to a newspaper which has unintentionally defamed a person, to publish a full apology and correction.

In all these defences it is not difficult to perceive the attempt to hold a proper balance between the right to speak freely and the right to have one's reputation properly preserved and respected. Technically all defamatory statements which amount to libel are also criminal—so that a libel is always a criminal libel. Although this is the theory, in practice prosecutions are very rare. Prosecutions for a gross libel on a group of individuals or on a deceased person are two examples where criminal proceedings are a possibility.

Other limits which have been placed on the right of freedom of speech are in regard to the criminal law offences of blasphemy, sedition and obscenity. In practice prosecutions are infrequent but one can see the reasoning why limits should be enforced here since the ultimate risk, if no action is taken, is that a breach of the peace will occur.

A different kind of limit has been placed on freedom of speech by the use of censorship to prevent offence being given in plays and films; by the statutory ban on horror comics; and by the attempt to prevent the publication of obscenity under the guise of literature. (See the Obscene Publications Act 1959.)

A rarely invoked limit of freedom of speech, at least in peacetime, is the use of the Official Secrets Acts legislation to prevent the passing of state secrets to a possible enemy. Again the need for a limit of this kind is self-evident.

The press and the broadcasting organisations are also vitally concerned with this topic of freedom of speech. They have received certain advantages under the legislation touched on above, for example the qualified privilege and offer of amends defences, but they are also subject by statute to certain limits on their reporting in such matters as juvenile court cases, domestic proceedings and divorce petitions. Again the attempt to strike a balance between freedom and some right to privacy is apparent.

Other than for these various limitations there is an absolute right to freedom of speech.

7 QUALIFICATIONS TO THE LIBERTIES OF THE SUBJECT

In addition to the various qualifications to complete liberty which have so far been encountered in this chapter, there are certain other subjects which have long been recognised as imposing limits in their own particular sphere on the freedom of the individual. In order to complete the picture it will be necessary to consider these.

(a) Contempt of Court

The exalted status of the courts, derived as it is from the Monarch as the fountain of justice, has always meant that sanctions are available to enforce the orders made by the courts and also to deal with any misconduct committed towards the courts.

It is obviously a contempt of court to throw missiles at the judge as has happened on a number of occasions, but it is equally a contempt of court to fail to carry out the orders of the court. For example, an order to hand over certain documents or to stop a nuisance. A further form of contempt is to prejudice a pending court case by the publication of inadmissible evidence or similar information likely to influence a jury.

Not all the courts have full power to punish for contempt. The magistrates have no power to commit for contempt at all. They must refer the matter to the High Court which will act on their behalf. The county court judge is limited to a punishment of three months' imprisonment or a £20 fine. The High Court and Appeal Court judges have however a complete discretion where they find this offence proved and the normal remedy is to commit the offender to prison indefinitely until such time as he is prepared to apologise and "purge" his contempt. At one time criticism was expressed that the court was prosecution, judge and jury in the matter and since there was no appeal from the court's ruling it was alleged that this was a very undesirable state of affairs. By s. 13 of the Administration of Justice Act 1960, however, an appeal will now lie to the Court of Appeal from an order of a civil court judge dealing with a contempt, and to the Queen's Bench Divisional Court from such an order in a criminal matter. A further appeal is, with leave, possible to the House of Lords. No leave is necessary if the contempt was committed in and dealt with by an Appeal Court.

(b) Parliamentary Privilege

From its beginnings the High Court of Parliament had attached to it special rights or privileges which it developed into a rigid and fully recognisable system as time passed. Then as the supremacy of Parliament became more and more settled, particularly at the end of the seventeenth century with the establishment of constitutional monarchy, so with it the privileges of Parliament came to be recognised by the courts as exceptional rights pertaining to an exceptional body. In just such a similar way the courts accepted and continue to accept the peculiar rights belonging to the monarch as the royal prerogative. On the other hand, although the courts acknowledge the existence of these parliamentary privileges they will not allow the range of such privileges to be extended.

(i) *Formal privileges.*—The privileges of the House of Commons are claimed by tradition by the Speaker at the opening of every new Parliament—as "the ancient and undoubted privileges" of that House; and these privileges are "most readily granted and confirmed" by the Lord Chancellor speaking for the Crown. Those which are specifically claimed are:

(i) the legal right of freedom of speech in debate

(ii) the legal right to have freedom from arrest

(iii) the right to have collective access to the Crown through the Speaker

(iv) that the Crown will place a favourable construction on the deliberations of the Commons

The first two privileges call for some explanation; the right of freedom of speech means that no action in law can be brought against a member of the House for statements made in the course of debate, i.e. absolute privilege attaches to speeches and this plea would be a good defence to an action for Defamation; the freedom from arrest does not mean that Members can escape the law. It means that no Member can actually be arrested within the precincts of Parliament and further that no arrest for civil debt can take place within forty days of a sitting. Arrest for civil debt is uncommon anyway and this privilege is of historical interest only. No protection is afforded against arrest for a criminal offence.

(ii) *Informal privileges.*—Other privileges of the House of Commons which are not formally claimed but which nonetheless exist are:

    (i) the right to regulate its own constitution

    (ii) the right to take exclusive cognisance of matters arising within the House

    (iii) the right to punish members and strangers for contempt

    (iv) the right to impeach, *i.e.* accuse of treason

    (v) the right to control finance

(iii) *The courts and parliamentary privilege.*—There was for a very long time a major conflict between Parliament and the courts over the question of parliamentary privilege. The courts sought always to contain the field of privilege and to make such privilege subject to the law. Parliament would have none of it and insisted on its right to conduct its affairs and to make law for itself accordingly.

The leading case on the subject is *Stockdale* v. *Hansard* (1839). An action for defamation was brought in the courts, the defamatory matter being in a report published under the authority of the House of Commons. The defendant pleaded the orders of the House, and the House itself stated that the matter fell within its own privilege. The Queen's Bench Divisional Court refused to accept this interpretation and decided that parliamentary privilege was not applicable. The plaintiff thus succeeded.

The next difficulty was that when, under the court judgment execution was levied, the House of Commons committed first Stockdale for contempt and then the two sheriffs who had levied execution. The court on an application for a writ of *habeas corpus* by the persons so imprisoned held that it could not question the parliamentary privilege to commit for contempt. Thus the Commons had the better of the conflict.

Although this particular set of circumstances was dealt with in the Parliamentary Papers Act 1840, nothing has been done to ensure that so undesirable a conflict could not recur. The courts acknowledge the existence of parliamentary privilege and will define the limits of that privilege: but within its limits Parliament is completely free to declare its own privilege and to punish for contempt. The principle of punishment is the same as in the case of contempt of court, but at least in the case of contempt of court there is now a right of appeal. If the House of Commons decides that there has been a breach of parliamentary privilege it can, without hearing him, commit the person concerned to imprisonment and he has no

right of appeal.   Clearly this is a substantial qualification to the
liberty of the individual and although such action is rare the very
existence of such power is extremely undesirable.

The present procedure, where a member considers that a bieach
of privilege has occurred, is for him to raise the matter in the House
of Commons and have it referred to the Committee of Privileges
There is no shortage of examples but the following instances are
among the more important:

In 1956 the editor of the *Sunday Graphic* in the course of a controversial article published the telephone number of a certain Member
of Parliament advising its readers to let the member know their
views. The member's telephone was put out of use by the number of
incoming calls. This action on the part of the editor was held to be a
contempt of Parliament and he was severely reprimanded.

In 1960 another member who raised in the House the distribution
of fascist propaganda leaflets by leaving them in telephone kiosks
received a threatening letter from the organisation which warned
him of "the possibility that in the resurgent Britain of tomorrow you
and your fellow renegades will face trial for complicity in the
coloured invasion and Jewish control of our land". This letter also
was held to be a breach of privilege as an attempt by improper
means to deter a member from the performance of his parliamentary
duties.   A repeat performance occurred in 1964 when members
received a letter containing the same threat if they supported the
Race Relations Bill then before Parliament. Again it was held to
be a breach of privilege but one not calling for any action.

The House was seen in its worst light in 1956 when it reacted
hastily to criticism of itself over the petrol rationing scheme brought
about by the closure of the Suez Canal. Suggestions that the scheme
was unduly favourable to politicians caused the newspaper editors
concerned to be found guilty of contempt. The editor of the *Romford
Recorder*, one of those concerned, complained that he was not even
permitted to defend himself.

The principle which underlies these decisions is the age-old
justification for censorship that criticism which holds the House up
to public obloquy "is calculated to diminish the respect due to it and
so lessen its authority." In fact as some members have pointed out
the respect due to the House will increase when less attention is paid
to the trivialities which are sometimes raised as alleged breaches
of privilege. An interesting article on the subject—"The misuse of the
question of privilege in the 1964-65 session of Parliament" by

Colin Seymour-Ure appeared in the magazine "Parliamentary Affairs" for autumn 1965.

In conclusion it ought also to be said that the House of Lords enjoys similar privileges, but it is much less common for arguments on privilege to occur in this House. The particular privilege of trial by peers, i.e. a right for a peer to be tried in the House by his fellow peers, was abolished by the Criminal Justice Act 1948: it had become of doubtful advantage.

(c) Crown Privilege

(i) *Definition.*—As might be expected the law has had to pay special regard to the position of the Crown. This is because, formally, the reigning monarch, as Head of State, is "the fountain of justice", and so the courts are the Queen's courts, and the judges are the Queen's judges. It would thus not be possible for the monarch to break the law—hence the maxim "the Queen can do no wrong"—nor for the courts to issue orders operative against their creator.

This long-standing immunity of the Crown from legal process came to be extended to the central Government departments of State too, since, as was seen in chapter 2, the ministers are "Her Majesty's Ministers" and all civil servants are directly employed by the Crown. This meant that a breach of contract by a ministry, or a tort committed by a civil servant would not give rise to a legal liability. The full effects of this Crown immunity were gradually qualified by a system of *ex gratia* payments, but this arrangement could not be justified in the changed conditions of the twentieth century. Feeling increased over a long period of time that this unrealistic and arbitrary right should be limited by Parliament. A draft bill was produced but many years elapsed before it became law as the Crown Proceedings Act 1947.

(ii) *Crown Proceedings Act* 1947.—Under the provisions of the Crown Proceedings Act 1947 the general position is that, whilst the maxim "the Queen can do no wrong" remains, government departments can be sued like ordinary litigants in contract and in tort. Some reservations were expressed in the Act, for example, an injunction cannot issue against the Crown although a declaratory order is possible; and no execution will be levied against the Crown. In both instances Parliament was prepared to assume that the departments would abide by the court's finding without the need for such express sanctions as are necessary when the litigants are private individuals.

Certain exceptional rights or privileges nonetheless remain. Special immunity attaches to the loss of postal packets or for certain other wrongs committed by post office employees. Similarly there is no legal liability to persons serving in the armed forces and suffering injury as a result of the actions of other members of the armed forces. The only remedy here is the statutory pension entitlement which the injured man will have.

(iii) *Privileged documents.*—In the procedural field a government department may refuse to produce documents on the grounds of "the national interest": for example in *Duncan* v. *Cammell Laird* (1942), an action brought by personal representatives of persons drowned in the accidental loss of the submarine Thetis, the Crown refused to allow Cammell Laird the builders to produce documents and drawings which might have explained the accident. This was during the war and was done on account of the national interest since the construction of similar submarines was on the secret list. In these circumstances the failure to produce the documents was justified; but in certain later cases the same claim was made in circumstances which were quite different and much less justified.

In *Ellis* v. *Home Office* (1953) a prisoner in Winchester prison alleged that he had been seriously assaulted by another prisoner. When the case was brought the Home Office successfully claimed privilege for medical and police reports about the prisoner who was alleged to have committed the assault. Two years later in *Broome* v. *Broome* (1955), a divorce case, the War Office successfully claimed privilege for documents which were in its possession dealing with the welfare work of officers associated with the Services.

(iv) *Continuing conflict.*—These decisions set off considerable academic and judicial criticism since in both the cause of justice was impeded by the claims made, and in neither case could the national interest be said to be affected by the withholding or publication of the information in question. As a result in 1956 and in 1962 the government, through the Lord Chancellor, announced a number of qualifications to the grounds on which crown privilege would, in future, be claimed.

Nonetheless the privilege remains and from time to time the courts are put in considerable difficulty by such claims: that expressed by Lord DENNING, M.R., in *Re Grosvenor Hotel London* (*No. 2*) (1965) is a clear statement of one view. He said:

> "The objection of a minister, even though taken in proper form, should not be conclusive. If the court should be of opinion

that the objection is not taken in good faith, or that there are
no reasonable grounds for thinking that the production of the
documents would be injurious to the public interest, the court
can override the objection and order production. It can, if
it thinks fit, call for the documents and inspect them itself so
as to see whether there are reasonable grounds for withholding
them: ensuring, of course, that they are not disclosed to anyone
else. It is rare indeed for the court to override the minister's
objection, but it has the ultimate power, in the interests of
justice, to do so. After all, it is the judges who are the guardians
of justice in this land: and if they are to fulfil their trust, they
must be able to call upon the minister to put forward his reasons
so as to see if they outweigh the interests of justice."

(v) *Conway* v. *Rimmer.*—The controversy has just been given a
fresh impetus by the majority decision of the Court of Appeal in
Conway v. *Rimmer* (1967). A former probationary police constable
in suing a former police superintendent for alleged malicious
prosecution sought to have access to four reports on him made during
his probationary training and also a report concerning the criminal
investigation sent by the police superintendent to the chief constable.
The police constable plaintiff had been acquitted on a charge of
stealing a torch. The Home Secretary claimed privilege on the
grounds that production of such documents would be injurious to
the public interest. The majority in the Court of Appeal held that
the court was bound by the *Duncan* v. *Cammell Laird* case and that
"an objection duly taken in proper form on behalf of the Crown to
the production of a document on the ground that disclosure of its
contents would be contrary or injurious to the public interest was
final and that in such a case the court had no power to inspect the
document or to decide whether the Crown's objection should in the
circumstances be sustained or over-ruled." (*per* DAVIES, L.J.)
Leave was given for an appeal to the House of Lords and it is very
much to be hoped that this takes place.

Even then however it is safe to predict that conflict will continue
because the two interests are so obviously opposed. On the one hand
is the minister's view of the public interest and the proper function-
ing of the public service, and on the other hand is the interests of
justice as seen by the individual parties. In these circumstances the
one sure conclusion is that no hard and fast rule is possible.

Appendix A

Some Sources of Law Illustrated

On the following pages are set out four documents, namely an Act of Parliament, a statutory instrument, a Ministry circular and a law report, each of which is an example of a "source of law", (see p. 29, above). These illustrations reproduce the first page or two of the document in its original form in order to show its actual appearance.

In addition these particular sources have been selected because all of them relate to a matter of some importance in Public Law, namely the procedure to be followed at inquiries held under the Town and Country Planning Act 1962. Under s. 23 of that Act a person who is aggrieved by the refusal of a local planning authority to grant planning permission may appeal to the Minister who must appoint an inspector to hold an inquiry at which arguments are presented by the aggrieved person and the authority. On the basis of the inspector's report the Minister will decide whether to uphold or reject the appeal.

The procedure to be followed by inquiries is laid down by the Tribunals and Inquiries Act 1958 (see p. 114, above) and the illustration on p. 174 shows the first page of that Act. At the top of the page is the short title, by which the Act is commonly known, and below the royal coat of arms follows the chapter number of the Act. Each Act is given a chapter number, roughly in the order in which they appear, beginning with No. 1 for the first Act of the year. Below the chapter number comes the "long title" of the Act which indicates its general purpose. At the end of the long title is the date on which the Act received the royal assent and so became law. This is followed by the words of enactment and thereafter the provisions of the Act are set out (see pp. 39, 41, above).

By s. 7A of this Act (which was added by s. 33 of the Town and Country Planning Act 1959) "The Lord Chancellor, after consultation with the Council [on Tribunals], may make rules for regulating the procedure to be followed in connection with statutory inquiries held by or on behalf of Ministers; . . ." Accordingly on 16th March 1965 the Lord Chancellor made the Town and Country Planning (Inquiries Procedure) Rules 1965, the first page of which is illustrated on p. 175. It will be seen that the Rules have been issued in the form of a statutory instrument as required by the Statutory Instruments Act 1946 (see pp. 39 and 57, above) and the number of the instrument is S.I. 1965, No. 473.

These Rules replaced similar Rules made in 1962 and accordingly at the time they came into force the Ministry of Housing and Local Government issued a circular, No. 25/65 dated 31st March 1965 (see pp. 176, 177) addressed to all local planning authorities drawing attention to the new Rules and explaining how they differ from the previous Rules.

Circulars are not themselves a source of law but are a means whereby a Ministry may offer advice and supply information to local authorities. However, in so far as they explain and advise on how new statutory provisions should be administered and enforced, and as the advice is almost invariably followed by local authority officials, they do have an important practical effect on the operation of the law.

Rule 13 (1) of the Town and Country Planning (Inquiries Procedure) Rules 1965 deals with the notification to the parties of the Minister's decision on the appeal and lays down that he "shall notify his decision, and his reasons therefor, in writing to the appellant . . .; and where a copy of the appointed person's [*i.e.* the inspector's] report is not sent with the notification of the decision, the notification shall be accompanied by a summary of the appointed person's conclusions and recommendations." The illustration on pp. 178, 179, shows the first two pages of the report of a case in which the High Court quashed the decision of the Minister (see p. 131, above) because he did not comply with these provisions. (The case actually concerns rule 11 of the earlier 1962 Rules but this rule is identical with rule 13 of the 1965 Rules).

The report is in the usual style of a modern law report and appears on p. 696 of Vol. 3 of the *All England Law Reports* for 1966, and in legal books this reference is abbreviated, following the name of the case, as: [1966] 3 All E.R. 696. The name of the case, the court and the date are followed by the "catchwords" (indicating briefly the subject matter of the case) and the "headnote", which is the reporter's summary of the facts of the case and the court's decision, followed by a reference to the relevant passages in Halsbury's Laws of England and a note of the only case referred to by the judge. The rest of the report is taken up by a statement of the background of the case and (beginning on p. 697) the judgment, in which the judge gives the reason for coming to his decision.

CHAPTER 66

An Act to constitute a Council on Tribunals; to make further provision as to the appointment, qualifications and removal of the chairman and members, and as to the procedure, of certain tribunals; to provide for appeals to the courts from decisions of, or on appeal from, certain tribunals; to require the giving of reasons for certain decisions of tribunals and Ministers; to extend the supervisory powers of the High Court and the Court of Session; to abolish certain restrictions on appeals from the Court of Session to the House of Lords; to make further provision with respect to the appointment and qualifications of General Commissioners of Income Tax, and provision for the payment of allowances to General and Additional Commissioners; and for purposes connected with the matters aforesaid.   [1st August, 1958]

BE it enacted by the Queen's most Excellent Majesty, by and with the advice and consent of the Lords Spiritual and Temporal, and Commons, in this present Parliament assembled, and by the authority of the same, as follows:—

1.—(1) There shall be a council, entitled the Council on Tribunals,— Council on Tribunals.

   (*a*) to keep under review the constitution and working of the tribunals specified in the First Schedule to this Act (being the tribunals constituted under or for the purposes of the statutory provisions specified in that Schedule), and, from time to time, to report on their constitution and working;

   (*b*) to consider and report on such particular matters as may be referred to the Council under this Act with respect to tribunals other than the ordinary courts of law, whether or not specified in the First Schedule to this Act, or any such tribunal;

1

STATUTORY INSTRUMENTS

1965 No. 473

TRIBUNALS AND INQUIRIES

The Town and Country Planning (Inquiries Procedure) Rules 1965

Made - - - -	*16th March* 1965
Laid before Parliament	*22nd March* 1965
Coming into Operation	*1st April* 1965

I, Gerald, Baron Gardiner, Lord High Chancellor of Great Britain, in exercise of the powers conferred upon me by section 7A of the Tribunals and Inquiries Act 1958(a) and of all other powers enabling me in this behalf and after consultation with the Council on Tribunals, hereby make the following Rules :—

Citation and Commencement

1.—(1) These Rules may be cited as the Town and Country Planning (Inquiries Procedure) Rules 1965.

(2) These Rules shall come into operation on 1st April 1965 but, save as provided in rule 17, shall not affect any application referred to the Minister or appeal brought before that date.

Application of Rules

2.—(1) These Rules apply—

(*a*) to local inquiries caused by the Minister of Housing and Local Government or by the Secretary of State for Wales to be held for the purpose of applications for planning permission referred to him under section 22 of the Town and Country Planning Act 1962(b) and appeals to him under section 23 of that Act and (to the extent provided in rule 15) to hearings before a person appointed by the Minister or by the Secretary of State, as the case may be, for the purpose of any such application or appeal ;

(*b*) to local inquiries caused by the Minister of Land and Natural Resources or by the Secretary of State for Wales to be held for the purpose of applications for consent referred to him under a tree preservation order and appeals to him under such an order and (to the extent provided in rule 15) to hearings before a person appointed by the Minister or by the Secretary of State, as the case may be, for the purpose of any such application or appeal, subject to the following modifications, that is to say—

(i) rule 4 shall not apply and the references in these Rules to section 17 parties shall be omitted ;

(ii) references to development shall be construed as references to the cutting down, topping, lopping or wilful destruction of trees ;

(iii) references to permission shall be construed as references to consent ;

(a) 6 & 7 Eliz. 2. c. 66.   (b) 10 & 11 Eliz. 2 c. 38.

MINISTRY OF
HOUSING & LOCAL GOVERNMENT
WHITEHALL, LONDON, S.W.1

31st March, 1965

SIR,

TOWN AND COUNTRY PLANNING (INQUIRIES PROCEDURE) RULES 1965
(S.I. 1965 No. 473)

1. I am directed by the Minister of Housing and Local Government to draw the Council's attention to the above-mentioned rules which have recently been made by the Lord Chancellor. Copies are available from H.M. Stationery Office.

2. These rules come into operation on 1st April, 1965, but do not affect applications referred to the Minister before that date. The rules revoke the Town and Country Planning Appeals (Inquiries Procedure) Rules 1962 (S.I. 1962/1425) which were substantially similar in so far as they applied to appeals for planning permission and to appeals for consent to the display of advertisements. (The Appendix to Circular No. 42/62 contained detailed advice on those rules. Any appeal to which they applied and which has not been determined by 1st April will be continued under the new rules.) A new provision (Rule 6(6)) enables the Minister to require an applicant or appellant to serve on the planning authority, the Minister and others directly concerned a written statement of the submissions which he proposes to put forward at an inquiry; and another (Rule 10(7)) enables the Inspector to take into account written representations or statements received before the inquiry from any person.

3. The scope of the new rules is wider, however, in that they cover also inquiries which arise out of applications for consent to the cutting down, etc., of trees in respect of which a tree preservation order has been made, or for consent to the execution of works on buildings in respect of which a building preservation order has been made.

4. In each of these classes, as well as the classes that were covered by the 1962 rules, the new rules cover two kinds of inquiries and hearings: those held on "called-in" applications, where the Minister exercises his power to have an application referred directly to him at first instance; and those held on appeals, where the local planning authority refuses permission or consent, and the applicant appeals to the Minister.

5. The opportunity has been taken in drafting the new rules of replacing references to the Town and Country Planning Act 1947 by references to the corresponding provisions of the Town and Country Planning Act 1962 (which has superseded the Act of 1947).

6. Account has also been taken of the transfer of certain functions from the Minister of Housing and Local Government to the Minister of Land and Natural Resources and to the Secretary of State for Wales. It will be noted that the rules therefore cover certain inquiries held on behalf of those Ministers as well as inquiries held on behalf of the Minister of Housing and Local Government.

7. Rule 16 contains adaptations of the rules in regard to Greater London made necessary by the re-allocation of planning functions in the Greater London area are consequent upon the London Government Act 1963.

I am, Sir,

Your obedient Servant,

A. MacC. ARMSTRONG,

Assistant Secretary.

The Clerk of the Authority.

Local Authorities
Joint Boards and Committees
England and Wales.

[P6/42/07]

NOTE: In Wales and Monmouthshire, any communication about this Circular should be addressed to the Secretary, Welsh Office, Cathays Park, Cardiff.

696   ALL ENGLAND LAW REPORTS   [1966] 3 All E.R.

GIVAUDAN & CO., LTD. *v.* MINISTER OF HOUSING   A
AND LOCAL GOVERNMENT AND ANOTHER.

[QUEEN'S BENCH DIVISION (Megaw, J.), Apr. 25, 26, 27, May 5, 1966.]

Town and Country Planning—Appeal—Permission for development refused—
Appeal to Minister—Notification of decision—Reasons so obscurely stated
as not to be good and sufficient reasons—Minister's decision dismissing   B
appeal quashed—Town and Country Planning (Inquiries Procedure) Rules,
1962 (S.I. 1962 No. 1425), r. 11 (1).

An application for planning permission was refused by the local planning
authority on three grounds. The applicants appealed to the Minister of
Housing and Local Government, who appointed an inspector to hold a local
inquiry. The inspector set out his conclusions in paras. 61-68 of his   C
report in which, after stating that the effect of a Bill (later enacted) might
require consideration, he dealt with the three grounds and found in favour of
the applicants on two of the grounds and against them on the third. He
recommended, on the basis of the adverse conclusion, that the appeal should
be dismissed. The Minister, in para. 3 of his letter notifying his decision on the
appeal and his reasons therefor, set out what appeared to be intended as a   D
summary of paras. 61-68 of the report, omitting, however, a passage crucial to
the inspector's conclusion on one of the grounds of objection on which he had
found in favour of the applicants. Paragraph 4 of the Minister's letter stated
merely that he agreed with the inspector's conclusions, without identifying
which of those conclusions, and accepted his recommendation. A copy
of the inspector's report was enclosed with the letter. The Minister dismissed E
the appeal. On an application to quash the Minister's decision, it was conceded by the Minister that the conclusions referred to in para. 4 of his letter
were not simply the whole of paras. 61-68 of the report and that the Bill
mentioned in the report was irrelevant to the appeal.

Held: it was impossible to be certain to what conclusions of the inspector
para. 4 of the Minister's letter referred, and indeed the letter was so obscure F
and would leave an informed reader in such a substantial doubt as to the
Minister's reasons and as to what matters he did or did not take into account
that the letter did not give the " good and sufficient reasons " which r. 11
(1)* of the Town and Country Planning Appeals (Inquiries Procedure)
Rules, 1962, required; accordingly the Minister's decision dismissing the
appeal to him would be quashed (see p. 698, letters A, C and E, p. 699,   G
letter F, p. 700, letter G, and cf., p. 701, letter C, post).

Per CURIAM: there can be no objection to the inclusion by reference in
the Minister's statement of reasons, of the inspector's conclusions, provided
that those conclusions are, in themselves, sufficiently clearly and unam-
biguously expressed (see p. 699, letter E, post).

[As to the Minister's duty to give the reasons for his decision, see 37 HALS-   H
BURY'S LAWS (3rd Edn.) 198, para. 311, note (*s*) and SUPPLEMENT to vol. 37,
para. 311A, 3; and for a case concerning the giving of reasons, see DIGEST
(Cont. Vol. A) 18, *242a.*

For the Tribunals and Inquiries Act, 1958, s. 12, see 38 HALSBURY'S STATUTES
(2nd Edn.) 212.]

Case referred to: I
Poyser and Mills' Arbitration, Re, [1963] 1 All E.R. 612; [1964] 2 Q.B. 467;
[1963] 2 W.L.R. 1309; Digest (Cont. Vol. A) 18, *242a.*

Motion.

This was a motion, by notice dated Sept. 15, 1965, as amended, by the applicants, Givaudan & Co., Ltd., pursuant to s. 179 of the Town and Country Planning Act, 1962, for an order quashing the decision of the first respondent, the
Minister of Housing and Local Government, dated Aug. 6, 1965, whereby he

_____
* The terms of r. 11 (1) are set out at p. 698, note (1).

Q.B.D. GIVAUDAN & CO. *v.* MINISTER OF HOUSING etc. (MEGAW, J.) 697

A dismissed an appeal by the applicants against the refusal of the second res-
pondents, Caterham and Warlingham Urban District Council, to permit the
erection of an office, flavours and stores building on land being part of the
applicants' existing factory at Godstone Road, Whyteleafe. The grounds of the
application were that the decision of the Minister was not within the powers
of the Act of 1962 and further that the relevant requirements had not been
B complied with whereby the interests of the applicants had been substantially
prejudiced. The notice set out five matters which it was alleged that the Minister
took into account and which were alleged to have been irrelevant, four matters
which he did not take into account which were alleged to have been relevant
and five allegedly relevant requirements which had not been complied with.
Paragraph 3 (e) of the amended notice is set out at p. 698, letter A, post, and
C the Minister's letter embodying his decision at p. 698, letter G, to p. 699,
letter E, post. The relevant facts are stated in the judgment.

Sir Derek Walker-Smith, Q.C., and *A. B. Dawson* for the applicants.
Nigel Bridge for the Minister.
The second respondent was not represented.

Cur. adv. vult.

D May 5. MEGAW, J., read the following judgment in which he stated the
nature of the motion and continued: The proposed building was intended to
be used partly for offices, partly for storage and partly for blending materials,
all in connexion with the business carried on by the applicants on the site. That
business is the manufacture and blending of chemicals for such articles as per-
fumes and soaps, foods and tooth-paste. In view of the conclusion which I
E have reached, I do not find it necessary to set out at length the facts and background matters, recorded in the inspector's report, which were developed in
argument before me in some detail.

The local authority (the second respondent), acting on behalf of the planning
authority, Surrey County Council, refused the application to erect the building
F on three grounds. They were: first, that the erection of the building would
constitute over-intensive development of the site and be detrimental to the
amenity of the neighbouring residential properties; secondly, that, having regard
to the nature of the existing and future processes and the difficulty of adequately
preventing the emission of fumes and smells, the further growth of Givaudan &
Co., Ltd.'s (the applicants') activities on the site in the manner and to the extent
G proposed should not be permitted; and, thirdly, that there would be inadequate
car-parking space at the factory as a whole, if the new building were to be erected.
This refusal by the planning authority having been notified on Aug. 7, 1964, the
applicants by notice dated Sept. 8, 1964, appealed to the Minister. He directed
that a local inquiry be held, and the inquiry was held on Mar. 9 to 11, 1965.
On May 14, 1965, the inspector submitted a long report to the Minister, recommending that on planning merits the appeal be dismissed. By letter dated
H Aug. 6, 1965, the Minister notified the applicants' solicitors that he dismissed the
appeal, and he made an order accordingly.

The applicants, being aggrieved by the order, now apply to the court under
s. 179 of the Town and Country Planning Act, 1962, to quash the order. The
notice of motion sets out a large number of grounds, in respect of which it is
alleged that the order is not within the powers of the Act of 1962 and in respect
I of which it is alleged that there has been a failure to comply with the relevant
requirements which ought to have been observed and that the applicants'
interests have been substantially prejudiced thereby. It is asserted for the
applicants that on the true construction of the Minister's letter of Aug. 6, 1965,
incorporating by reference the inspector's report or parts thereof, or on the basis
of inferences properly to be drawn therefrom, it appears that the Minister took
into account, to the prejudice of the applicants, matters which were not relevant,
and failed to take into account matters which were relevant. The applicants
further contend, by para. 3 (e) of their amended notice of motion, that the

How a Case is Decided

This Appendix consists of an extract from a judgment delivered in the Court of Appeal in the case of *R. v. Paddington Valuation Officer, ex parte Peachey Property Corporation*, [1966] 1 Q.B. 380; [1965] 2 All E.R. 836. This extract has been chosen because it provides a good example of how the judges apply the doctrine of judicial precedent in a case in order to dispose of the questions of law that arise.

This extract has also been chosen because it provides a very full consideration of the grounds on which the prerogative orders of *mandamus* and *certiorari* may issue (see Chapter 5).

The case was argued before the Court of Appeal between March 30 and April 9, 1965. On June 1 the judges delivered judgment in which two of them (Lord DENNING, M.R., and SALMON, L.J.) held that the appeal should be dismissed and the other judge (DANCKWERTS, L.J.) held that it should be allowed. Accordingly the appeal was dismissed. The following is taken from the judgment of Lord DENNING:

"The applicants, Peachey Property Corporation, Ltd., own a great number of houses and flats in London and elsewhere. In particular they own a big block of flats known as Park West, near Marble Arch. There are 629 flats there. It was designed and built for the purpose of flats. Hence these flats were called throughout the case "purpose-built flats". This serves to distinguish them from flats in converted houses. There are many Georgian and Victorian houses in the Paddington area which were designed and built as single dwellings, but owing to changing times have been converted into flats and maisonettes. They are called "flats in converted houses".

The applicants complain that they and their tenants in Park West have been badly treated in regard to the rates on their purpose-built flats. They say that the first respondent, the valuation officer for Paddington on the one hand has rated *the purpose-built flats* at *too high* a figure: and on the other hand has rated *the flats in converted houses* at *too low* a figure. They say that this is because he has prepared the whole of the valuation list on the wrong footing. The valuation list for Paddington contains 31,656 dwellings. The applicants say that it is all bad. They ask the court to issue an order of certiorari, so as to quash the list altogether; and they ask the court to issue an order of mandamus, so as to order the first respondent to make a new list. The issue thus raised is of great importance. It is acknowledged that the valuation officers for the whole of London have prepared their lists on a similar footing to the Paddington list. It may be that the rest of England has also been prepared in like manner. If the Paddington list is bad, so also may be valuation lists up and down the country.

Before I deal with the facts, I propose to deal with the law: for it helps to see the issues involved.

I. What is the proper remedy?

The first question is whether the remedy by certiorari or mandamus is open at all, seeing that there is a remedy given by statute. The statutory remedy is contained in s. 40 to s. 49 of the Local Government Act, 1948, as amended by s. 1 and s. 3 of the Lands Tribunal Act, 1949. Summarised, the remedy is this: the applicants, if they are aggrieved, are entitled to make proposals for the alteration of the valuation list. They can propose alterations, either downwards or upwards. On the one hand, they can ask that the values on their own Park West flats be reduced. On the other hand, they can ask that the values on other people's flats in converted houses be increased. If the valuation officer does not agree to the proposals, the applicants can appeal to the local valuation court. If that court decides against them, they can appeal to the Lands Tribunal. The decision of the Lands Tribunal is final, save that on a point of law there is an appeal to the Court of Appeal: and thence, in turn, with leave, to the House of Lords.

Counsel for the first respondent contended strongly before us that, as Parliament had provided this specific remedy, the applicants ought to go by it. There was a code of procedure, he said, specially designed by Parliament, to deal with grievances such as these. That was their proper course. Indeed, their only course. Such specific remedy being given, they could not resort to the remedy of certiorari or mandamus. He supported this contention by reference to *Pasmore* v. *Oswaldtwistle Urban District Council* (1898), *R.* v. *City of London Assessment Committee* (1907) and *Stepney Borough Council* v. *John Walker & Sons, Ltd.* (1934). Now these cases certainly warrant the proposition that, if the applicants were attacking the assessment of any one *particular* hereditament, or any small *group* of hereditaments, such as all the houses in a particular terrace, their only remedy would be that statutory remedy. By which I mean that, if and in so far as they are attacking *particular* assessments within a *valid* valuation list, they must go by the remedy which Parliament has provided, namely, to make proposals to alter those assessments. But if and in so far as they are attacking the valuation list itself and contend that the *whole list is invalid* (as they do), then I do not think that they are confined to the statutory remedy: for the simple reason that the statutory remedy is in that case nowhere near so convenient, beneficial and effectual as certiorari and mandamus. I suppose that in theory the applicants might make proposals for the alteration of every one of the 31,656 hereditaments in the list, but that would in practice be impossible. Counsel for the first respondent conceded this; he suggested, however, that a few test cases might be taken, and proposals could be made for altering those few assessments and a decision given by the Lands Tribunal. But one side or the other might not agree on what should be taken as test cases. And in any case the procedure would be most deficient because there could be no discovery against the occupiers. I am, therefore, of opinion that the existence of the statutory remedy is no bar to this application. The case falls within the general principle that the jurisdiction of the High Court is not to be taken away without express words; and this applies both to the remedies by certiorari and mandamus (see *Re Gilmore's Application* (1957)), and also to the remedy by declaration (see *Pyx Granite Co., Ltd.* v. *Minister of Housing and Local Government* (1960)).

II. Is the applicant a "party aggrieved"?

The second question is whether the applicants are persons aggrieved so as to be entitled to ask for certiorari or mandamus. Counsel for the first respondent contended that they are not persons aggrieved because, even if they succeeded in increasing all the gross values of other people in the Paddington area, it would not make a pennyworth of difference to them. Strange as it may seem, owing to the way expenses are borne in the County of London, the rate poundage of Paddington would remain the same even if the assessments of the flats in converted houses were greatly increased. If the assessments were increased by £1,000,000, the rate poundage would be reduced by a penny. I do not think that grievances are to be measured in pounds, shillings and pence. If a ratepayer or other person finds his name included in a valuation list which is invalid, he is entitled to come to the court and apply to have it quashed. He is not to be put off by the plea that he has suffered no damage, any more than the voters were in *Ashby* v. *White* (1703). The court would not listen, of course, to a mere busybody who was interfering in things which did not concern him. It will listen to anyone whose interests are affected by what has been done, just as it did in *R.* v. *Thames Magistrates' Court, Ex parte Greenbaum* (1957), and in *A.-G. of Gambia* v. *N'Jie* (1961). So here it will listen to any ratepayer who complains that the list is invalid.

III. Are certiorari and mandamus available?

The third question is whether certiorari and mandamus are

available in respect of a valuation list. The Divisional Court [in this case] thought that they were; and counsel for the first respondent did not contend otherwise. The first respondent is a public officer entrusted with a public duty. He has legal authority or power to determine questions affecting the rights of subjects, namely, to assess the values of hereditaments. This power carries with it the duty to act "judicially", which means, I think, fairly and justly in accordance with the statute. If he declines or fails to carry out this duty, he is amenable to mandamus; and the list itself is liable to be quashed on certiorari: see *R. v. Electricity Comrs., Ex parte London Electricity Joint Committee Co.* (1924); *R. v. Manchester Legal Aid Committee, Ex parte R. A. Brand & Co., Ltd.* (1952); *Ridge v. Baldwin* (1964).

IV. The resulting chaos.

The fourth question is what is to happen if the valuation list is quashed. It was said that it would be a nullity from the beginning. The rating authority would have to go back to the 1956 list which was based on 1939 values: see s. 34 (2) of the Local Government Act, 1948. It would be necessary, it was said, to unravel all the assessments and payments since Apr. 1, 1963. The result would be chaos. I do not accept this at all. It is necessary to distinguish between two kinds of invalidity. The one kind is where the invalidity is so grave that the list is a nullity altogether. In which case there is no need for an order to quash it. It is automatically null and void without more ado. The other kind is when the invalidity does not make the list void altogether, but only voidable. In that case it stands unless and until it is set aside. In the present case the valuation list is not, and never has been, a nullity. At most the first respondent—acting within his jurisdiction—exercised that jurisdiction erroneously. That makes the list voidable but not void. It remains good until it is set aside.

'It bears no brand of invalidity on its forehead. Unless the necessary proceedings are taken at law to establish the cause of invalidity and to get it quashed or otherwise upset, it will remain as effective for its ostensible purpose as the most impeccable of orders:'

see *Smith v. East Elloe Rural District Council* (1956) per Lord RADCLIFFE. No doubt if the list is invalid altogether, certiorari must in due course go to quash it. But I see no reason why a mandamus should not issue in advance of the certiorari: cf. *R. v. Cotham* (1898). If the existing list has been compiled on the wrong footing the court can order the first respondent to make a new list on the right footing. (The passage of time is no bar: for counsel for the first respondent concedes that the requirement for it to be prepared by Dec. 31, 1962, was directory only and not mandatory.) Once the new list is made and is ready to take effect, the court can quash the old list. In that case everything done under the old list will remain good. The rates that have been demanded and paid cannot be recovered back. For it is a general rule that where a voidable transaction is avoided, it does not invalidate intermediate transactions which were made on the basis that it was good: see the cases collected in *Director of Public Prosecutions* v. *Head* (1959). By this solution, all chaos is avoided. The existing list will remain good until it is replaced by a new list: and then it will be quashed by certiorari. But I think that then it must be quashed. You cannot have two lists in being at the same time. The Divisional Court took the view that certiorari was a necessary pre-requisite to mandamus. I do not think that it is a pre-requisite. Certiorari will be necessary some time, but only when the new list is ready to take effect. So we have to be sure that certiorari will lie.

V. On what grounds will certiorari lie?

The fifth question is the most important of all. On what grounds will certiorari lie to quash a valuation list? The Divisional Court thought that it would only lie for excess of jurisdiction or error of law on the face of the list. But the word "jurisdiction" in this context has innumerable shades of meaning. Some advocates are prone to say that, whenever a tribunal or other body decides wrongly, it exceeds its jurisdiction. It has only jurisdiction, they say, to decide rightly, not to decide wrongly. This is too broad a view altogether. I would say that, if a tribunal or body is guilty of an error which goes to the very root of the determination, in that it has approached the case on an entirely wrong footing, then it does exceed its jurisdiction. Thus where magistrates refused to issue summonses, in spite of the evidence, because they thought that it was undesirable for the prosecution to go on, it was held that was tantamount to declining jurisdiction: see *R.* v. *Adamson* (1875). And when the Board of Education failed to determine the questions asked of them, but answered another not put to them, it was held that they had declined jurisdiction: see *Board of Education* v. *Rice* (1911). Again when licensing justices refused an application on a ground not open to them, it was held that they had exceeded their jurisdiction: see *R.* v. *Weymouth Licensing Justices, Ex parte Sleep* (1942). These cases confirm me in the view which I expressed in *Baldwin and Francis, Ltd.* v. *Patents Appeal Tribunal* (1959):

'. . . if a tribunal bases its decision on extraneous considerations which it ought not to have taken into account, or fails to take into account a vital consideration which it ought to have taken into account, then its decision may be quashed on certiorari and a mandamus issued for it to hear the case afresh.'

But how does this principle apply in regard to the *whole* of a valuation list (which can be quashed on certiorari) in contrast to *particular* assessments in the list (in which there is statutory remedy by appeal)? The error must be one which affects the list as a whole, or a large part of it, and not merely particular hereditaments in it. It seems to me that if the valuation officer prepared the list on entirely the wrong basis, contrary to the directions in the statute, it could be quashed. An instance can be found in the books. Suppose in preparing a new list, he simply took the old list and, instead of assessing each hereditament individually, he multiplied the old values three times all the way through. Clearly the list could be quashed: see *John Stirk & Sons, Ltd.* v. *Halifax Assessment Committee* (1922); *Ladies' Hosiery and Underwear, Ltd.* v. *West Middlesex Assessment Committee* (per SCRUTTON, L.J.) (1932). Again if he took the actual rents paid without making any adjustments (for rates, repairs, services or furniture), clearly the list would be bad. So also if he disregarded the statutory test of 'what a hypothetical tenant might reasonably be expected to pay' and substituted an arbitrary scale of values based on a preconceived formula (such as so many shillings per square foot according to the type of hereditament) then again the list would be quashed. These instances would all be cases where, in the words of the Divisional Court,

'. . . the valuation officer has misdirected himself on some fundamental matter or matters which so vitiate the value of his work that it must be regarded as worthless.'

In short, there must be error which goes to the root of the list or a large part of it.

The Facts

So much for the law. I turn now to the facts to see if this list is vitiated by fundamental error . . ."

Lord DENNING then went on to consider the facts of the case and to hold that although there had been inconsistency of treatment between purpose-built flats and other flats there was no fundamental mistake of law going to the root of the valuation list as a whole, and so *certiorari* to quash the list would not be granted.

Appendix C

The Judges' Rules

NOTE

The origin of the Judges' Rules is probably to be found in a letter dated October 26, 1906, which the then Lord Chief Justice, Lord ALVERSTONE, wrote to the Chief Constable of Birmingham in answer to a request for advice in consequence of the fact that on the same Circuit one Judge had censured a member of his force for having cautioned a prisoner, whilst another Judge had censured a constable for having omitted to do so. The first four of the present Rules were formulated and approved by the Judges of the King's Bench Division in 1912; the remaining five in 1918. They have been much criticised, inter alia for alleged lack of clarity and of efficacy for the protection of persons who are questioned by police officers; on the other hand it has been maintained that their application unduly hampers the detection and punishment of crime. A Committee of Judges has devoted considerable time and attention to producing, after consideration of representative views, a new set of Rules which has been approved by a meeting of all the Queen's Bench Judges.

The Judges control the conduct of trials and the admission of evidence against persons on trial before them: they do not control or in any way initiate or supervise police activities or conduct. As stated in paragraph (*e*) of the introduction to the new Rules, it is the law that answers and statements made are only admissible in evidence if they have been voluntary in the sense that they have not been obtained by fear of prejudice or hope of advantage, exercised or held out by a person in authority, or by oppression. The new Rules do not purport, any more than the old Rules, to envisage or deal with the many varieties of conduct which might render answers and statements involuntary and therefore inadmissible. The Rules merely deal with particular aspects of the matter. Other matters such as affording reasonably comfortable conditions, adequate breaks for rest and refreshment, special procedures in the case of persons unfamiliar with the English language or of immature age or feeble understanding, are proper subjects for administrative directions to the police.

JUDGES' RULES

These Rules do not affect the principles

(a) That citizens have a duty to help a police officer to discover and apprehend offenders;

(b) That police officers, otherwise than by arrest, cannot compel any person against his will to come to or remain in any police station;

(c) That every person at any stage of an investigation should be able to communicate and to consult privately with a solicitor. This is so even if he is in custody provided that in such a case no unreasonable delay or hindrance is caused to the processes of investigation or the administration of justice by his doing so;

(d) That when a police officer who is making enquiries of any person about an offence has enough evidence to prefer a charge against that person for the offence, he should without delay cause that person to be charged or informed that he may be prosecuted for the offence;

(e) That it is a fundamental condition of the admissibility in evidence against any person, equally of any oral answer given by that person to a question put by a police officer and of any statement made by that person, that it shall have been voluntary, in the sense that it has not been obtained from him by fear of prejudice or hope of advantage, exercised of held out by a person in authority, or by oppression.

The principle set out in paragraph (e) above is overriding and applicable in all cases. Within that principle the following Rules are put forward as a guide to police officers conducting investigations. Non-conformity with these Rules may render answers and statements liable to be excluded from evidence in subsequent criminal proceedings.

RULES

I. When a police officer is trying to discover whether, or by whom, an offence has been committed he is entitled to question any person, whether suspected or not, from whom he thinks that useful information may be obtained. This is so whether or not the person in question has been taken into custody so long as he has not been charged with the offence or informed that he may be prosecuted for it.

II. As soon as a police officer has evidence which would afford reasonable grounds for suspecting that a person has committed an offence, he shall caution that person or cause him to be cautioned before putting to him any questions, or further questions, relating to that offence.

The caution shall be in the following terms:—

" You are not obliged to say anything unless you wish to do so but what you say may be put into writing and given in evidence."

When after being cautioned a person is being questioned, or elects to make a statement, a record shall be kept of the time and place at which any such questioning or statement began and ended and of the persons present.

III—(*a*) Where a person is charged with or informed that he may be prosecuted for an offence he shall be cautioned in the following terms:—

"Do you wish to say anything? You are not obliged to say anything unless you wish to do so but whatever you say will be taken down in writing and may be given in evidence."

(*b*) It is only in exceptional cases that questions relating to the offence should be put to the accused person after he has been charged or informed that he may be prosecuted. Such questions may be put where they are necessary for the purpose of preventing or minimising harm or loss to some other person or to the public or for clearing up an ambiguity in a previous answer or statement.

Before any such questions are put the accused should be cautioned in these terms:—

"I wish to put some questions to you about the offence with which you have been charged (*or* about the offence for which you may be prosecuted). You are not obliged to answer any of these questions, but if you do the questions and answers will be taken down in writing and may be given in evidence."

Any questions put and answers given relating to the offence must be contemporaneously recorded in full and the record signed by that person or if he refuses by the interrogating officer.

(*c*) When such a person is being questioned, or elects to make a statement, a record shall be kept of the time and place at which any questioning or statement began and ended and of the persons present.

IV. All written statements made after caution shall be taken in the following manner:—

(*a*) If a person says that he wants to make a statement he shall be told that it is intended to make a written record of what he says.

He shall always be asked whether he wishes to write down

himself what he wants to say; if he says that he cannot
write or that he would like someone to write it for him, a
police officer may offer to write the statement for him.
If he accepts the offer the police officer shall, before
starting, ask the person making the statement to sign, or
make his mark to, the following:—

"I, ..., wish to make a statement.
I want someone to write down what I say. I have been
told that I need not say anything unless I wish to do so
and that whatever I say may be given in evidence."

(*b*) Any person writing his own statement shall be allowed to
do so without any prompting as distinct from indicating
to him what matters are material.

(*c*) The person making the statement, if he is going to write it
himself, shall be asked to write out and sign before writing
what he wants to say, the following:—

"I make this statement of my own free will. I have
been told that I need not say anything unless I wish to
do so and that whatever I say may be given in evidence."

(*d*) Whenever a police officer writes the statement, he shall
take down the exact words spoken by the person making
the statement, without putting any questions other than
such as may be needed to make the statement coherent,
intelligible and relevant to the material matters: he shall
not prompt him.

(*e*) When the writing of a statement by a police officer is
finished the person making it shall be asked to read it and
to make any corrections. alterations or additions he
wishes. When he has finished reading it he shall be asked
to write and sign or make his mark on the following
Certificate at the end of the statement:—

"I have read the above statement and I have been
told that I can correct, alter or add anything I wish.
This statement is true. I have made it of my own free
will."

(*f*) If the person who has made a statement refuses to read it
or to write the above mentioned Certificate at the end of
it or to sign it, the senior police officer present shall record
on the statement itself and in the presence of the person
making it, what has happened. If the person making the
statement cannot read, or refuses to read it, the officer
who has taken it down shall read it over to him and ask

him whether he would like to correct, alter or add anything and to put his signature or make his mark at the end. The police officer shall then certify on the statement itself what he has done.

V. If at any time after a person has been charged with, or has been informed that he may be prosecuted for an offence a police officer wishes to bring to the notice of that person any written statement by another person who in respect of the same offence has also been charged or informed that he may be prosecuted, he shall hand to that person a true copy of such written statement, but nothing shall be said or done to invite any reply or comment, If that person says that he would like to make a statement in reply, or starts to say something, he shall at once be cautioned or further cautioned as prescribed by Rule III(*a*).

VI. Persons other than police officers charged with the duty of investigating offences or charging offenders shall, so far as may be practicable, comply with these Rules.

Index